HEAVEN:
33 Stories *from a* Real Place

Jim Harwell

Bridge Books
Atlanta   Chicago   Nashville

Bridge Books
4487 Post Place
Nashville, Tenn. 37205

Heaven: 33 Stories from a Real Place. Copyright © 2015 by Jim Harwell

All rights reserved, including the right to reproduce this book or portions thereof in any form whatsoever. For information, address:
Bridge Books Subsidiary Rights Department
4487 Post Place
Nashville, Tenn. 37205

For information about Bridge Books products, books, packages, and special discounts for bulk purchases, please contact Bridge Books at 615-873-0882 or info@bridgebooks.org.

Scripture references are taken from the New King James Version.© Thomas Nelson, Inc. 1992.

Cover designed by Dean Tomasek, Ray King and Douglas McFerrin

Manufactured in the United States of America

10 9 8 7 6 5 4 3 2 1

Library of Congress

ISBN-13: 978-0-9855-9433-6
ISBN-10:   0-9855-9433-0

From *Heaven: 33 Stories from a Real Place*...

"They placed me at the feet of the most glorious Being I could ever imagine. A crown of pure light rested on His head, and hair as white as snow fell upon His shoulders. No words could begin to describe His splendor... I was totally overawed by Him. His goodness, tenderness, and love overwhelmed me. I bowed down."[1]

-Marietta Davis

"He looked down at me. He had such beautiful eyes. I'll never forget those eyes. They were so large and full of meaning—and kindness and forgiveness and compassion. Everything you would want to see in Jesus' face was there."[2]

-Lorraine Tutmarc

"I looked into Jesus' eyes... they looked like wells of living love. It seemed as if one could see a half mile deep into them, and the tender look of His love is indescribable. As I looked into His face and into His eyes, I fell at His feet."[3]

-Kenneth Hagin

"I felt I had everything I ever wanted to have. I was everything I had ever intended to be. I was arriving at where I had always dreamed of being."[4]

-Betty Malz

Eby calls his visit "unutterable... indescribable... spiritually resplendent... and most ecstatically moving."[5]

The scene was "gorgeously unsurpassable in its beauty," with the foliage having a radiance. It was a great outdoors of mountains, trees, flowers, music, and sweet smells. Forests of symmetrical trees unlike anything on earth covered the foothills on each side. Every tree was tall, graceful, perfect, unblemished... Rolling hills under cloudless skies seemed to stretch for miles. The skies were a new color, an iridescent white-gold light. The valley floor was gorgeous. Stately grasses with perfectly straight blades were mixed in with ultra-white, four-petalled flowers on stems two feet tall, with a touch of gold at the centers.[6]

-Richard Eby

She looked into his eyes, which were loving and clear as blue water, yet piercing. It was like she was mirrored in his eyes . . . There was a heavenly illumination that made his hair light red, his eyes bluish and transparent, and his skin a light gold color . . . 'There is no way to describe his coloring. It is like another world's color. It's the Shekinah glory, iridescent golden light glowing through him.'[7]

-Valvita Jones

As he turned around, he saw Jesus Christ. The glory about Him moved toward Roberts and came upon him, engulfing him. Roberts fell to his knees, and tears began to stream from his eyes, running down his face. Jesus said, "I want to give you a tour through heaven, this place I have made for all who believe, because I love you so much."[8]

As he said this, tears again poured down Roberts' face. To Roberts, Jesus' presence is so tender that your joy turns to tears.

He said repeatedly, "I love my people so much. Why do people not take me at My word? Do they not know that I have all power in heaven and on earth to back up what I said? It is so easy. I made it so simple. If people would just take me at My word, I will do what I said."[9]

-Roberts Liardon

Richard saw a crystal city made entirely of glowing lights of different types. The lights gave off rays of glory brighter than the sun. The whole city was filled with tall buildings . . . Some were round, and one was shaped like a diamond. There were choirs and angels singing from the heights. Richard still remembers weeping with adoration and joy at seeing and hearing these inexpressible things.[10]

Jesus walked onto the stage to thunderous praise, worship, and adoration. The Lord looked at people lovingly... 'You could feel the Shekinah glory love that came out of Him. It was awesome ... words fail.'[11]
　　　　　　　　　　-Richard Sigmund

Suddenly... there stood Jesus... glory and power billowed all around Him... His piercing eyes were beautiful... the tenderness in His eyes' is beyond a writer's description. The loveliness of the Blessed Savior was awe-inspiring and wonderful.[12]
　　　　　　　　　　-Mary Baxter

A voice said: "Come with me into the Throne Room where the secrets of the universe are kept!"[13]

Chrioni said to him: "You can never comprehend the depth of God's love because it is too great!"[14]
　　　　　　　　　　-Roland Buck

"Jesus spoke with a voice that relayed the same love his glance transmitted to me—such gentleness and tenderness. Once you hear it, you will never forget it."[15]
　　　　　　　　　　-Gerald Landry

The light was so intense, he had to look away and keep looking down... He is so big—you can't describe Him in a dimension ... The form of God's body is somewhat like energy and spirit. The power, the energy-like smoke of God, covers all around the chair of the throne itself... There was a massive amount of energy, power, smoke, and noise there.[16]
　　　　　　　　　　-Jesse Duplantis

Jesus was dressed in a white robe down to His feet, with a golden sash around His chest. His eyes were gleaming and welcoming. His hair was white as snow, thick, and hanging down below His shoulders... His face oozed with love that was tangible and real... His face is radiant and inviting.[17]
　　　　　　　　　　-Maurice Maelo

Also from Bridge Books:

Confessions of a Practical Joker
Cats n' Dogs: A Tail of Two Opposites
Sidelines
Funny Thing About Baseball
Funny Thing About Football
Funny Things About Sports
Quotes, Jokes and Anecdotes

Contents

Foreward, Introduction

Chapter 1	Marietta Davis	1
Chapter 2	Rebecca Springer	14
Chapter 3	Lorraine Tutmarc	21
Chapter 4	George Ritchie	24
Chapter 5	Kenneth Hagin	31
Chapter 6	Betty Malz	35
Chapter 7	Deborah O'Donnell	39
Chapter 8	Gary Wood	41
Chapter 9	Richard Eby	46
Chapter 10	Rhoda Jubilee Mitchell	56
Chapter 11	Valvita Jones	61
Chapter 12	Roberts Liardon	64
Chapter 13	Richard Sigmund	73
Chapter 14	Mary Baxter	97
Chapter 15	Roland Buck	115
Chapter 16	Gerald Landry	124
Chapter 17	Ian McCormick	127
Chapter 18	Yong Gyu Park	130
Chapter 19	Jesse Duplantis	132
Chapter 20	Don Piper	143
Chapter 21	Choo Thomas	146
Chapter 22	Maurice Maelo	149
Chapter 23	Khalida Wukawitz	154
Chapter 24	Bill Smith	157
Chapter 25	Mary Neal	159
Chapter 26	David Taylor	162
Chapter 27	Michael McCormick	166
Chapter 28	Colton Burpo	168
Chapter 29	Dean Braxton	173
Chapter 30	Marvin Besteman	177
Chapter 31	Eben Alexander	181
Chapter 32	Crystal McVea	186
Chapter 33	Bob Misst	188
	Notes	192
	Bibliography	197

HEAVEN:
33 Stories *from a* Real Place

Foreword

ARE YOU READY for the ride of your supernatural life? Are you ready for a journey into the spirit world, a place full of wonder, beauty, joy, peace, miracles, angels, answers, mysteries, and more than you can imagine? This book will take you there.

If you're ready to go on a journey with 33 normal, everyday people who have actually visited heaven and experienced eternity, keep on reading. It's an incredible, almost unbelievable, miraculous look into the spirit world—into heaven and what is on the other side, what is waiting for us after we die.

After reading it, I'm amazed and almost speechless. It's supercharged! This is totally different from any other spiritual book you've ever read.

It's full of first-hand accounts of heaven, without all the "preaching" and "teaching" many books have. It is 33 testimonies that have incredible, profound teaching, revelation, and spiritual truth that can transform your life. Moreover, it contains the awe-inspiring, supernatural, unbelievable experiences these 33 people had in heaven and in the spirit world—the eternal world is that is eternally more important than our dress rehearsal on earth.

Get ready to ride through the heavens, tour the third heaven, see and meet Jesus Christ and mighty angels, meet and speak to patriarchs of the faith, see mansions and incredibly large buildings of all kinds, see the wondrous natural beauty of heaven, and be left speechless.

Now I realize that earth is a faint reflection of heaven, which is filled with breathtakingly beautiful landscape, full of trees, mountains, rivers, grass, flowers, neighborhoods, vilages, and homes, amidst millions of people and angels and more.

That's all just the beginning. The accounts are filled with profound revelations regarding spiritual things, answering many of the questions we all have regarding faith, eternity, and the things of God. Every story will stir your faith and arouse hope.

The author Jim Harwell is a respected writer and journalist. But his real passion is Jesus and the Spirit-filled journey. He's been involved in ministry on four continents, written several books, and spent years researching and preparing this one, with the purpose of helping people realize how awesome Jesus Christ is.

This collection is also intended for anyone and everyone who wants to know whats on that other side.

Enjoy the ride.

Elizabeth Drennan

Introduction

The afterlife. It's a topic most of us want to know about. After all, we will all have to face it at some point.

What if 33 people, most of whom died and came back to life, experienced heaven and offered to tell you about their experiences? What if they told you about the supernatural places they visited and the things they saw, experienced, and learned there?

That is what this book is all about.

After spending more than 20 years researching this topic, I feel this book is something everyone can benefit from. Whether you are a skeptic, a Muslim, a Hindu, an Agnostic, a Buddhist, an Atheist, a Christian, or a follower of any other faith or belief system, this book is intended for you.

This book is intended to present 33 people's first-hand accounts of the afterlife and heaven, without frills, preaching, teaching, or anything else related to the boring, awful aspects of religion or anything related to it.

In fact, this book has nothing to do with religion and everything to do with relationship.

It is intended to cut through all the unneeded extras and present amazing testimonies of heaven and the spirit realm, accounts that will inspire faith, hope, and love and encourage even the most cynical and disillusioned people to reconsider their stances. I think you'll be amazed at the revelation, truth, and answers to deep and longtime mysteries mankind has wondered about and debated for centuries.

The accounts are simple yet profound, fun yet serious, entertaining yet convicting, revealing yet concealing, and more.

One of the purposes of it is to explore the wonder and the reality of God.

First, the wonder. It is truly wonderful to find out, learn about, and/or know that there is a heaven, a place of glory, beauty, and wonder.

Second, the reality. On the objective side of things, the 33 stories are from a very wide assortment of men, women, and children, from many different countries, covering a time span of more than 150 years.

Through it all, there is a parallel structure and truth and many common denominators. Many of the people saw similar things, learned the same truths, and came away with similar memories. Parallel truth is a fancy way of saying that there is repetition of the same ideas, experiences, and similar concepts.

Some people may believe these accounts are only "dreams" or fantasies. Test it out yourself. Even if you don't believe in this type of thing—in heaven, hell, the spirit realm, afterlife, angels, demons, and supernatural things—read these stories, compare them, and decide for yourself.

Could two people living 150 years apart just coincidentally have similar experiences during a near death experience?

Could 33 people coincidentally see, hear, and experience very similar things and at times even the same things in heaven—and yet each and every one have a unique experience at the same time?

Could adults decades ago and a young boy in the early 2000s—a boy who did not know how to read or write—just randomly learn similar truths in heaven?

In some ways, I deliberately tried to write this book as a journalist objectively covering and fully exploring the topic: people who have been to heaven.

I spent hours and hours researching, exploring, and strategizing about how to present every individual's experience, whether it was Deborah O'Donnell's, the shortest chapter, or Richard Sigmund's, the longest.

The chapters are generally chronological, from Marietta Davis' circa 1850 visit to Bob Misst's in 2010.

At the same time, I also wore another "hat" during the decades-long preparation of this book. I am a Christian and have worked in ministry for both an evangelical and a charismatic ministry. I have seen "both sides" of the modern protestant church. These writings are an extension of my life's work and have been many years in creation.

I spent years just gathering the stories. I found books on different continents while working there. I have interviewed sons and daughters of people who have been to heaven. I have traveled thousands of miles to hear these people speak, teach, and minister.

Consider that much of the content in the accounts is also confirmed in the Bible, which has more than 580 references to heaven.

According to the Bible, it takes two or three witnesses (or more) to confirm a truth (Deuteronomy 19:15 and 2 Corinthians 13:1). In other words, one witness or person regarding a certain truth is not enough. There must be at least two and preferably three—or more. The more the better. Here we have 33 witnesses to heaven.

Jim Harwell

ONE

Marietta Davis

MARIETTA DAVIS LIVED during the first half of the 1800s in Berlin, New York, USA, near Albany, the state capital.

At the age of 25, in about 1850, she had a supernatural experience with God, published it, and became widely known in her community. The book was in print 100 years later.

Just before Davis' experience, there was a revival in her hometown of Berlin. Seven months after the revivial, Davis fell into a trance for nine days, during which she visited heaven. No one could rouse her from her trance.

Tragically, Marietta died seven months after her visits to heaven and hell, just as she predicted.

Her book's unusual, formal, flowery language made it difficult to read in modern times. Therefore two ministers, husband and wife Dennis and Jolene Prince of Melbourne, Australia, rewrote it in easier to read, modern language, preserving the original intent of the account.

At the time of her visit to heaven, Davis did not have much interest in spiritual things.

Suddenly, Marietta saw a vast, bottomless area beneath

her and an endless, trackless space around her. She was reeling, with strange unidentifiable objects floating around her. It was like a wild dream.

A brilliant light appeared above her, and her whole being was bathed in a glorious glow. This light transformed into the most glorious being she had ever seen. She was wearing a crown of clustered jewels of light. She held a cross in her left hand and a saber of light in her right hand. As the being came toward her, the saber's light touched Marietta, and a whole new world of sensations filled Marietta's being, sweeping away fears and uncertainties.

As Davis wondered who this being was, the response was, "I am the Angel of Peace. I have been sent to show you what happens to humans when they leave this world . . ."[1]

Marietta's mind was racing.

Her experience started somewhat gradually, with the walls of her house disappearing. Then her amazing experiences began.

When discussing her supernatural visits, Marietta explains: "There is simply no way on earth to fully describe the things beyond earth. Our words even spoil the beauty and perfection of the heavenly things that are out there."[2]

The angel asked Davis to look back, whereupon Davis saw herself motionless body, with her friends frantically shaking her to wake her up.

The angel explained to Marietta that they were seeing the human view of life and that the true picture of what happens after death was hidden from them.

Davis explained that for a long time, she has wondered greatly about what happens to people when they die. Now, unexpectedly and remarkably, she was on the brink of a monumental discovery about these issues.

"Marietta, you have been given a special favor to learn about these things," said the angel. "Look up there."[3]

Davis looked above herself and saw a vast, shining heavenly place, brighter by far than the sun. Brilliant, dazzling light radiated from it, shooting across the skies.

The angel explained that the people there live in unalloyed happiness, where there is no night, sorrow, or death, no sin or pain, no suffering of any kind. However, the angel said she must also show Davis things not so pleasant.

A new scene appeared before her, vivid and graphic, showing the people of earth dying and approaching eternity. Davis noticed spirits of different kinds gathered around all the dying forms—some by evil spirits, some by holy angels. The people were in the gateway of death.

People were attracted to spirits of a similar moral nature: evil and unholy with evil spirits, good people with holy angels.

The angel led Davis away and said, "Look at all these planets, the rolling heavens, the suns and systems of suns. See how they move in complete silence and perfect harmony. It is a massive expanse of universes built in infinite wisdom. Happy, holy people live in these—at different stages of development and different degrees of spirituality. These people will never die again."[4]

The angel touched Davis' eyes, and Davis immediately saw spirits of pure light passing by and travelling at the speed of thought. The angel said they were serving angels, who love to go on trips of mercy. They are protectors and messengers to people.

An angel passed by carrying a baby, explaining that he was taking it to the infants' heaven in the Paradise of Peace.

Davis and the angel stopped on a plain filled with trees with shady branches, laden with fruit. Birds were singing, their melodies delightful, the sweetest songs she had ever heard. The angel explained they were in the outer region of the spiritual paradise, where the trees, flowers, and birds are so pure and refined that humans cannot see them. They are experienced through spiritual senses.

The angel explained further that this outer region or boundary is the lower levels of the homes of the holy, the first place the redeemed go when they die. In this place, their guardian protectors teach them the basics of eternal life, such as about heaven and pure love. They see old friends and family.

Davis' eyes were opened further, allowing her to see many, many happy people moving through flowery landscapes. Davis wanted to join them, but the angel moved her forward and upward, through forests which became purer and more beautiful each moment.

Ahead Davis saw a domed pavilion of light, the gate to the City of Peace, according to the angel, who added, "You will meet your Redeemer."

As they got closer, a glorious group of angels gathered and spoke to Davis' angel, in a language Davis could not understand.

The gate, made of diamonds and jasper, opened and two angelic beings approached a trembling Davis and led her to the pavilion. Davis: "The sight of this perfect beauty and holiness was beyond description."[5] Davis fell to the ground under the conviction of her sinful state. The angels gently picked her up and carried through an elaborate doorway. Davis:

> "They placed me at the feet of the most glorious Being I could ever imagine. A crown of pure light rested on His head, and hair as white as snow fell upon His shoulders. No words could begin to describe His splendor ... I was totally overawed by Him. His goodness, tenderness, and love overwhelmed me. I bowed down ..."[6]

Jesus reached out His hand and lifted her up, saying "Welcome, My child." The sound of Jesus' voice penetrated deep inside her, filling her with a joy she could not describe. Jesus said, "Come for a while into the home of the redeemed," and to those around, "Make her welcome."

The gathering welcomed her and played an anthem, with the music sounding like a rush of many waters, filling the entire dome.

Someone Davis knew hugger her and said a big "Welcome!" as did many others. Davis could not describe them, except that they seemed to be "all mind, all light, all glory, all adoration, all love supremely pure, all peace, and calm serenity."[7]

The people talked freely with each other, but without sound, thought to thought and spirit to spirit. Ideas flowed, and Davis realized in heaven you could not hide anything. She realized that harmony was in everything—in speech, desire, songs, appearance, and more.

They sang a song of redemption, while Davis experienced the glory of the place.

Davis explains how she used to doubt heaven could be as wonderful as people claim it to be. She writes: "Rest assured, even the wildest imaginations of people do not begin to approach the reality/ and pleasures of that glorious place."[8]

Davis then spoke to a man she had known on earth, a man singing the praise of Immanuel, the Lamb of God.

The angel told Marietta to look up to the glory of the cross coming down, with redeemed spirit with it. Twelve people carried the cross, and the words "Patriarchs, Prophets, and Apostles" were written around them.

Above them, the words "Jesus of Nazareth, King of the Jews" was written.

Marietta was informed she was in heaven for a short time and would have to return to earth again, a thought that distressed her. The spirit who told her these things said that "All of heaven reveres the cross. Tens of thousands bow before it . . ."[9] Continuing, the spirit spoke about the countless, unseen guardian angels. She explained that the spirit appointed to watch over a person continually watches the human being.

The spirit continued: "There are many things preventing the light of heaven from reaching mankind, but the time is getting close when people will become more aware of the reality of this place . . . Man's final redemption is getting close."[10]

The spirit was female. She continued, telling Davis that Marietta would receive a tiny part of the joy that fills heaven and explaining that residents of heaven often kiss the cross.

In the distance, Davis heard "alleluias," sung by those who came out of the great tribulation.

Davis did not want to leave. The spirit told her to "be faithful . . . to the light given you."[11]

The spirit showed Davis a tall pyramid made of pearls and precious stones, set with diamonds in the form of crosses. Crowds were gathered around it. The pyramid had engraved names of those who spoke the truth of the gospel and received persecution and even death.

Three spirits stood on the pyramid: a patriarch, a prophet, and an apostle. The spirit explained that the three spirits would accompany the Son of Man when He returns to the earth. They will gather the selected people from the four winds, from the most distant part of earth and heaven.

The spirit said that books the three spirits held describe "the order of creation, the redemption of man, and the principles which govern the obedient."[12]

Two children approached Davis. One asked Marietta to tell the child's family on earth that he is free and extremely happy. The child said, "Our guardian angels take us to visit earth, but it is not at all like heaven."[13]

An angel went by, overwhelming Davis with his light and glory, which Davis could feel. The spirit explained that the angel is a guardian protector of infants and is commissioned to meet baby spirits as they leave earth and enter the spiritual world.

The angel breathed on Davis as if imparting life to her.

After this, Davis saw a vision of a woman grieving over her child's death. A man dressed in black solemnly spoke to her. The scene changed, and the woman was at a coffin at a funeral, with the man there as well. The child explained that this vision was of his own death, with the woman being his mother.

A voice called out, "Come up here!", and Davis and the

angel ascended in a chariot-like cloud through the interior of a tower with galleries. The walls seemed to be made of rainbows with beautiful colors and shine. Davis was filled with a deep sense of peace and delight.

They emerged on an aerial plain above the lofty dome of the central temple and could see the complete layout of the great city. The beauty was breathtaking. They could see the infants' Temple of Instruction, an architectural wonder on a soft lawn of lush, green grass, surrounded by majestic trees, fragrant flowers, and dancing fountains on marble channels and beds of golden sand. Some fountains gushed up high, streaming into basins which looked like diamonds, polished silver, or white pearl.

Trelliswork with a gateway surrounded the circular lawn, and a river flowed out of the gateway, with the fountains supplying the river.

Davis noticed that the city was divided into 144 great divisions, almost like suburbs of a large city. First, the river divided the city into 12 great divisions. From the center, the river flowed in a spiral course, making twelve very large curves and thus creating the 12 city divisions.

A wide avenue was on each side of the river. Straight streets began near the temple and radiated out to the 12 points on the outer boundary.

Davis gazed upon the city and its stately avenues and lost all sense of time and self awareness. She became absorbed in the splendor and complexity of the city and all it contained.

The buildings were extremely large and perfectly integrated with all the others. She writes:

> "The entire city gave the impression of being one garden of flowers, one grove of shady trees, one gallery of sculptures, and one sea of fountains. All of these, together with the buildings, formed an unbroken expanse of sumptuous architecture set in a surrounding landscape of matching beauty . . . the colored sky bathed every object in its incredible and

ever-changing shades."[14]

Then she noticed the inhabitants. The angelic multitude moved like a single melody, with one inspiring love, moving in one orderly plan. Their focus was the development of the children to perfection. The children were filled with holy love and a desire to grow in wisdom. Children were united to more mature children, loving to learn from them and devote themselves to unselfish acts of love.

The children went from beauty to beauty. Davis: "All above them was glory. All around them was loveliness. All within them was the melody of unfolding life, love, knowledge of heaven, adoration of the Savior, and the inspiration of eternal joy."[15]

Davis' female guide spoke and said that Davis would have to receive a sobering lesson. In a sudden and startling reversal, Davis left heaven and had a dreadful and agonizing experience in hell.

First, Davis descended and passed through a low and gloomy subterranean vault and thick folds of darkness. Dread consumed her as she shook with fear. As conflict arose in her heart, her thoughts shattered into utter chaos. A blue fire flash lit up the darkness, and grim specters floated by her, enveloped in fire. She felt horror and despair.

She writes: "Alone and in that dreadful place there are no means by which I can give even a faint idea of the agony of that moment."[16]

Her life flashed before her, with her conscience and previous doubts and skepticism condemning her. All her secrets were uncovered.

She was stunned as the words of the Savior echoed in her mind: "Men will have to give an account on the day of judgment for every careless word they have spoken" (Matthew 12:36).

Her erroneous views of Jesus (man, predestination, no hell and so forth) haunted her. She realized that she was not able to see him as He truly is: in His divine glory, with honor, majesty, and perfection, as Prince and Savior.

Just as she was giving up all hope, she saw Him reaching out His arms toward her, speaking with a voice of love, "Come to me." Yet, there was such a gulf between His holy place and her impure, fallen mind, she could not reach him.

A gloomy black veil rose up from below, and Davis began to descend rapidly. Eventually, she saw a vast unending plain filled with crowds of people, moving restlessly from place to place. They wore all kinds of clothing, cloaks, crowns, tiaras, jewelry, and gaudy clothing. Some worse helmets and headbands with feathers. The whole scene seemed artificial. They wore every kind of lavish garment, such as robes of royalty. There were tribal people with barbaric ornaments. Some wore ordinary clothes or ancient costumes. They all carried themselves with pomp and pride.

The people were laughing and shouting in amusement and revelry. They yelled obscenities, curses, and sarcasm. Some added in degrading language, backbiting and fake compliments and congratulations.

Disturbed, Davis moved slowly and cautiously. The trees around her gave off fiery blasts, with blossoms of flames. Objects around her caused her agony. The glare of the objects burned her eyes. The fruit she picked scorched her hand and seared her lips as she tried to eat it. The flowers gave off a stinking gas that cause severe pain in her nostrils.

She tried to find even a single drop of water. Fountains appeared, with small streams flowing into calm pools. But she realized the pools were just another deception, and the spray from the fountains felt like drops of molten lead. The flowing streams were like liquid metal, the pools like a fiery crucible.

Davis met a woman she knew on the earth. Possessing a brilliant external appearance, the woman explained the torment of being in hell, a disembodied spirit with a deep sorrow and agony that never goes away. She said: "Everyone who inwardly denies the Savior comes here when they die."[17] For her, the things she craves, she detests, and the things she delights in torture her. On earth, she had a proud, rebellious heart and sought pleasure without restraint.

The woman explained that the place they were in is "one great sea of perversion and depravity . . . lust and pride, hatred and greed, ambition and strife . . . The total effect is the combination of every evil."[18] She told Davis that if people on earth knew how awful their fate would be, they would prepare for eternity and even seek to extend their life to do so. She added: "Earth is a place of testing for everyone."

She emphasized that "your senses here are infinitely more acute . . . the awareness of suffering and the ability to suffer are far greater here."[19]

As she spoke, many hopeless beings had gathered around her, listening to her descriptions. Davis was filled with horror. The woman said this place was "just the surface of even deeper woes."[20] The woman sobbed, and another person told Davis to leave, as Marietta just being there reminded them of their lost opportunities. Nevertheless, the man who said this began to explain to Davis about why people on earth are attracted to sin and evil.

He said that man's spirit is difficult to perceive on earth, but when he dies, that spirit becomes the very basis of his existence. On earth, people believe there are no consequences of sin and that God is too good to punish someone for eternity. The man cried out in despair, urging Davis to warn people on earth about the terrible things waiting for those who continue to gratify their wrong desires.

Davis was then in a place of complete blackness called the Second Sphere. There she encountered an intellectual, a false teacher, and heartless worshipers.

Return to Heaven

Finally, and fortunately, Davis returned to heaven. The angel guide told her that Davis represented people who had not made up their minds about spiritial issues. The angel gave her advice about living righteously.

The angel pressed Davis' temple, and from a deep silence,

Marietta heard music that was "like angelic breath, like the inner and most holy life of the spirit," a transforming experience.[21]

When Davis tried to force herself into the music, rather than letting it flow through her, discord flared up and her sinful nature swept over her. Davis cried out to be hidden from the light, realizing she was unfit for paradise. The angel finally spoke, reminding her of how good God is to provide redemption to man. Moreover, the angel explained that God has arranged for spirits of similar nature to be kept together in the same place: good and evil in separate places. As John said, no unclean thing can enter the Holy City. (Revelation 21:27 and 22:11; Luke 16:26; 1 John 3:9-10)

The angel's words struck Marietta's heart like an arrow, and Davis began to weep. But the angel encouraged her, telling her that God's mercy is vast, and His redemption is available to everyone who wants it.

Davis heard the songs of the infants, filling the expanse and swelling into gentle waves, each infant glowing in holiness. A female spirit moved among the children, who watched her closely and sought to follow her example.

Next, a totally different scene was presented to the children. At times, dramatization is used to instruct the children, as real life scenes are presented to teach them about principles and past events. Davis explains that it is beyond her ability to explain everything used in this process: "It would also require volumes to contain it all, even if it could be written down."[22]

The lights dimmed, and a dramatic scene played out for everyone to see. It was a story of a lost man. As the scene closed, an angel addressed the children, explaining the scenes and story. He told the children that the gloomy place was earth, where people struggle with many sicknesses—physical, moral, and spiritual—but they cannot save themselves.

The angel then prayed to the Father to let the children have understanding and grace as they advance in their spiritual lives.

The next story was the story of God coming to earth as a man, the story of Jesus the Redeemer and Savior, also called the Bethlehem Story.

The next dramatization was the Justice-Mercy Conflict, a very moving and powerful depiction of the conflicting pull between justice and mercy. Justice was depicted as a mighty, all-powerful being. Destruction took place in the drama, and man had no hope. Mercy spoke and called out to God, pleading with the Almighty Creator to spare man. Mercy, a female, found a ransom for the sinners of earth: Jesus the Son of God and the His sacrifice on the cross.

The scene shifted to the Judas betrayal.

The children and angelic spectators were deeply moved. They cried out against the suffering Jesus endured. A company of angels appeared, a dazzling light going before them. A cherubim praised the Lord Jesus, the Redeemer of the earth. Mercy spoke to Justice, repeating John 3:16 and the hope Jesus brings to the world. An angel taught the children further about Jesus' sacrifice.

Justice stood on a cloud, holding the seven thunders, lightning and storms bursting from them, shaking the foundations of the earth, making men tremble in fear. In his left hand he held a scroll containing the law.

Mercy entered the storm, voicing the truth about Jesus becoming a man to identify with mankind.
Justice and Mercy agree that Jesus must suffer and become the Ransom.

Justice said: "Let all heaven agree, so that God will be all and over all, now, in the future, and forever."

The conspiracy against Jesus continued, with more dramatic scenes about the sacrifice of Jesus. Chapters 19 to 24 depict the betrayal, crucificion, death, and resurrection of Jesus the Savior.

The time was near for Davis to depart and return to earth. The children sang her a hymn, with Marietta feeling their love and the matchless worth of heaven. The angels and a spirit spoke encouraging words to her before the children circled around her. A person hugged her and then led two children to her. The two children asked Davis to tell the people on earth that the children are happy and have no sorrow and are waiting patiently for the arrival of their loved ones.

Then Jesus descended from a cloud, placing His hand on her head and speaking to her:

> "Child, it is important that you return. You have a commission. Be faithful to it. Whenever you have an opportunity, tell people what you have seen and heard. Fulfill your mission and, at the appointed time, angels will meet you at the gate of death and carry you to your home here in the kingdom of peace. Do not be sad. My grace will uphold you. In your sufferings you will be supported."[22]

Jesus placed a golden goblet on her lips. As she drank she was filled with new life and courage.

The angels carried Marietta in their arms to the gateway of the temple and sang praise to God. Davis descended to earth.

TWO

Rebecca Springer

REBECCA RUTER SPRINGER (1832-1904) was an author, wife, mother, and homemaker in the 19th century in Illinois and Indiana, USA.

She wrote the widely acclaimed book *Intra Muros*, also called *Within Heaven's Gates*, about her visit to heaven.

Springer was originally from Indianapolis, Indiana, USA, and her father was a Methodist minister. She was married to William McKendree Springer, an attorney and longtime political leader and activist. William served for more than 20 years in the Illinois House of Representatives and later represented Native American tribes in their efforts to preserve their lands.

Throughout much of her life, Rebecca dealt with health issues. When she was 36 years old, she and her family even went on a two-year trip to Europe to improve her health.

As a young woman and wife, Rebecca was on her deathbed for three weeks in Kentville, Canada, a small town in Nova Scotia 100 km northwest of Halifax, the capital. Today, Kentville has 6,000 residents.

While ill in Kentville, those in attendance tried to help her but did not provide proper assistance. She longed for her family and friends and cried out to Christ to be with her.

One day, she sensed someone in her small room. Unbelievably, it was her brother-in-law Frank who was deceased. He asked her if she was ready to leave. She was concerned about leaving her husband and young boy. Frank assured her she would return. So they departed, as Frank picked her up and carried her. Rebecca was relieved someone was caring for her.

Suddenly she was sitting in an opening covered with flowering bushes and small plants. She was standing on the softest green turf she had ever seen. The grass was filled with fragrant flowers.

She remembers seeing at least four types of flowers she knew on earth as well as some she did not know. The flowers were perfect, such as the heliotrope which were smooth and glossy. The flowers seemed to be inviting your admiration.

Rebeccas was in awe of her surroundings. Everything seemed perfect. The air was soft, balmy, and invigorating. The light was much different from sunlight. The light was golden, with a shining glory everywhere.

The field of perfect grass and flowers stretched out farther than she could see. There were majestic trees with hanging branches bearing blossoms and fruits of many kinds (Revelation 22:2).

People were everywhere. Under the trees, there were many groups of children happily playing. They were trying to catch brightly colored birds that were also playing. Happy and peaceful adults were walking nearby, wearing pure white clothing and even flowers.

There were beautiful homes and architecture with unique designs. She saw sparkling fountains in many places. A river flowed with crystal clear water.

Rebecca had forgotten about Frank, who had been watching her and said, "Well?"

They came to the river, which was lined with beautiful

stones. She noticed she was wearing the white.

Though she was concerned about drowning, she and Frank jumped in the river. Springer found she could breathe, talk, and see. Frank told her to run her hands over her face and through her hair, which produced a delightful feeling.

As soon as she got out, she was completely dry. Her clothing was whiter, and she felt more free, as if she could fly. Frank explained that the river washed away the influences of the earthly life and got her ready for heaven.

They walked on. Rebecca saw beautiful homes with large balconies, in styles she had never seen. The vines and flowers there were more beautiful than she could imagine. She heard happy people in the homes.

Frank explained they were going home. They came to a home of light gray marble and large trees. She was surprised to hear a familiar voice, her close friend Mrs. Wickham, who hugged Rebecca and planned to visit them later.

At the home, Frank officially welcomed Rebecca to her house. They walked upstairs and through large marble columns. They walked into the reception hall, which had an inlaid floor, windows, and a wide, low stairway.

He led her into another large room of polished gray marble. The walls and floors were covered with what looked like real roses of every type and color. When Rebecca tried to pick one up, she realized they were embedded in the walls.

Frank explained that a group of boys and girls, upon finding out the home was the Springers, had created the stunning artwork. The girls brought bouquets of roses and threw them over the floors and walls. The boys used tools to embed the flowers in the marble.

They then toured the library, filled with rare and expensive books, a stained glass window, and a writing desk, among other things. They discussed the books, some of which were written in heaven and some on earth. Rebecca realized that heaven was to be a place of increased knowledge and understanding.

Every room was distinct and perfect. Her personal rest

and study room was made with wood rather than marble. It contained ivory bookshelves and an ivory desk. The furniture was ivory with silver gray upholstery.

They walked through an open window onto a marble promenade with a staircase that wound down to the lawn. Trees branches with fruit hung close by. The fruit was delicious. She ate what looked like a pear, with juice running down her hands and clothes. But when she finished, her hands and clothes were as clean as before.

Now in the room filled with roses, Frank asked her who she would like to see. She replied that she wished to see her parents, who along with her sister walked toward her.

Rebecca continued to see loved ones. Her niece Mae, radiant and joyful, ran toward her. Mae praised Jesus and expressed her love for Him.

They arrived at a lake that was so glorious Rebecca could not look at it. It was smooth as glass and filled with flowers and tress. In the distance, she saw a city.

People were on the banks and in boats. Children and animals played around the lake with no fear or anxiety. Angels sang overhead. Rebecca wept. They both went hundreds of feet down into the lake, lied down, and the rose up with a current. Springer watched a panorama of colored lights.

Rebecca could hear music in the distance. Mae explained that the lake caught reflected both light and music. The lake had filled her with the divine life.

They visited Mrs. Wickham's beautiful home, getting a tour of it. Wickham's daughter played the musical instruments found in one of the rooms.

While Wickham was away for a moment, someone was at the door. It was Jesus!

He looked into her eyes with such love, she wept. They embraced, and Jesus wiped away her tears. He began to explain the mysteries of heaven. After talking, He arose to depart, telling her they would meet often. He laid His hands on her head to bless her.

Mrs. Wickham led Rebecca to the door, allowing

Springer to process her encounter with Jesus.
She returned home.

Rebecca reunited with a friend Mary Bates. They spoke about Mary's mother who was still on earth. They encountered four people, including Jesus. One look from Him lifted their spirits.

Frank told Rebecca they were going to hear Martin Luther and John Wesley speak. They went to the auditorium on a hill. It was a massive dome with columns.

The large hall had three sides of seating around the platform. The seats were made of polished cedar wood. The platform was made of marble, with purple curtains behind it. In the center of the platform, there was an altar made of pearl. The dome overhead was dark with gold carvings.

As they were seated, the audience was eagerly waiting, listening to the soft music from an invisible choir. Luther ascended the steps. He spoke with strength and intellect.

John Wesley followed, speaking about "God's Love."

After the talks, a silence fell upon the crowd. The purple curtains parted. Jesus walked in.

The crowd sang a hymn of praise to Him. The angel choir could even be heard. The glory of God filled the auditorium.

Jesus began to speak. His voice was sweeter than the choir of angels. She could find no earthly words to express what He spoke about. His subject was the link between life on earth and heaven and the wonderful duties of the redeemed.

Rebecca was reunited with Oliver, a brother-in-law. They went to his house and saw his grandchildren. Then she was reunited with her sister Lu, who looked radiant and about 30 years old.

She returned to the lake and got in, seeing the amazing colors again. She heard the bell in the city, and the waters responded to it. She floated a ways and found herself in a village that looked like Switzerland, though the village was far more beautiful.

There she saw and spoke to her friend Maggie, who was weaving draperies.

Springer happened upon a group of children sitting around Jesus, who help one tiny girl in His arms. He was telling them a story, as the kids were listening intently. The kids shouted at the end.

Frank asked her if she wanted to visit the city. She longed to. They got in a boat in the lake and went to the farthest shore. The boat went up to a marble terrace, the entrance to the city. They went up a hill and onto a broad street that led to the city. The street was paved with marble and other majestic stones. There were many people around.

Rebecca saw many buildings, similar to office, colleges, schools, stores, publishing houses, libraries, lecture halls, auditoriums, art galleries, and factories. She did see homes in the middle of the city; they were in the suburbs. The whole city was like a big garden and park, with homes here and there.

They went to the open country, walking through plains and meadows and into a vast forest. They then came to a great plain and saw an enormous temple with a dome, pillars, and walls. She fell to her knees in worship.

They silently walked up the pearl steps to enter the temple. They were in awe of the vast dome held up by three great pillars of gold. Much of the temple was made of pearl. A railing surrounded the platform on three sides. There was an altar of gold on the platform. Beneath the altar was a fountain, which was the source of the river of life.

Two people by the altar knelt with heads bowed. Four angels in white stood with golden trumpets in their hands. The draperies behind the platform glowed with a radiance like the sun. The temple was filled with the cloud of His glory. The trumpets sounded. The angelic choir sang, "Holy, holy, holy." They bowed their heads in silence.

They returned home. She noticed hearing songs from the earth. Frank explained that heaven was a continuation of the earth life without all the negatives.

Rebecca was also reunited with her aunt Ann and a friend Mary Green. She helped her father with a mission of reuniting a son with a mother in heaven. She was also reunited with her husband Will. Rebecca and Will set out to the glassy sea. It was glorious, with a brightness beyond description. There were boats representing the nations. An innumerable multitude of people stood on the shore. They were awaiting the arrival of friends and family.

Then Rebecca wondered if the care and uneasiness of earth had entered heaven. She realized she was back on earth, in the small room in Kentville, Canada.

THREE

Lorraine Tutmarc

LORRAINE TUTMARC (1906-1992) was given a glimpse of heaven in 1928 when she was 22 years old.

While pregnant with her third child, Lorraine had a miscarriage and developed serious health problems.

Up until her supernatural experience, Tutmarc had not been a spiritual person. She was a longtime resident of the Seattle, Washington, USA, area.

For three months Lorraine had suffered pain throughout her body and was almost too weak to move. Tutmarc had peritonitis which developed into blood poisoning. Since there were no antibiotics at that time, doctors told her they could nothing else for her.

One morning, while lying in her bed, she realized the pain was gone. She felt something strange happen, like she was lifted out of her body. She went to the upper corner of the room.

She looked back and saw her husband, the doctor, and a nurse gathered around her bed. Next she moved backward through the wall.

Tutmarc found herself in a black, very cold river up to her neck. A loud voice told her "This is eternity . . . You are lost!"[1] and explained that she was in the River of Death. It was God's voice. At this point in her life, she did not know Jesus Christ as Savior.

Then Jesus appeared.

She saw a light. Looking up at the light, she saw Jesus about four feet above her in an opening over her head. Everything else was black, but Jesus was brilliant and shining. The light coming from him was beyond description.

"He looked down at me. He had such beautiful eyes. I'll never forget those eyes. They were so large and full of meaning—and kindness and forgiveness and compassion. Everything you would want to see in Jesus' face was there."[2]

She noticed Jesus' compassionate face, penetrating eyes and the fact the He was not smiling but sad.

Looking at His pale ivory robe, she noticed a big blotch of red on his chest. Jesus told her, "This is the blood that I shed on the cross for your sins." Then, "Follow me." Lorraine responded, "I will!"[3]

Immediately, a brilliance came from Jesus. It was more than sunshine. A transparent gold light came from him and from his body.

When she took hold of Jesus' warm hand, Lorraine instantly felt the power of God go through her, though she did not even heard of the power of God. The power was like "sparks from smitten steel" from her head to her toes again and again.[4]

They both floated toward a wall, stopping near it. Lorraine looked up and saw a transparent wall, almost like shining, pure gold, as far as she could see in either direction.

Behind the wall, Lorraine knew there was much activity. She heard birds singing; millions of bells ringing and tinkling; humming; a choir singing in a perfect harmony in a minor key; and stringed instruments. She could smell flowers, with a fragrance like perfume on a gentle breeze.

Then, suddenly, Jesus was gone.

In an instant, she was back in her body.

Craig Gottschalk, Lorraine Tutmarc's grandson, also had a supernatural experience in the spirit realm.

At the age of 18, Gottschalk and his friends were heavily involved in drugs. One night after a party, he passed out and had a supernatural vision during his near death experience.

First he saw a video of his sinful life. He began falling down toward a place where he was tormented. He screamed to be saved, and Jesus took hold of him and pulled him back. There was then a tug-of-war for his soul, between Satan and Jesus. Finally, Jesus said he was going to save Craig because of his grandmother's constant prayers.

Next, Jesus showed Craig a stairway and taught him two lessons: that God is eternal, and that God's knowledge and wisdom have no end. Craig's conclusion is that God is infinite and knows infinitely.

Then Craig was taken to heaven. He was in a room so big he could not tell how large it was. He saw Jesus and the Book of Life as well as million of angels standing in perfect silence and reverence.

Jesus introduced Craig by his spiritual name and wrote it in the Book of Life, though Craig cannot remember the name. The angels rejoiced and sang and praised God.

The angels had solid bodies, though he could see about a half inch "into" their "skin" but not through the center part. They seemed very tall.

Jesus told Craig, "I'm going to send you back because I have work for you to do."[5] The last thing the Lord said to him was "Breathe," and Craig was back in his body and awake.

FOUR

George Ritchie

GEORGE RITCHIE (1923-2007) was a psychiatrist and medical executive, based primarily in Richmond, Virginia, USA.

During a long and successful career, he served the medical profession in numerous ways. He was in private practice for many years and was a past Director of Psychiatry at Towers Hospital. He was President of the Richmond Academy of General Practice and was Director of the Department of Psychiatry at a university.

As a young man, he died, spent time with Jesus, saw heaven, and came back to earth. The experience happened while he was a young U.S. Army enlistee during World War II.

In 1943, 20-year-old Ritchie was a tall, skinny, typical young man, living in Richmond. Like many young American men, he enlisted to serve in the army, despite having been accepted to attend medical college in Virginia.

In September of 1943, he was sent to Camp Barkeley, Texas, for basic training, where more than 250,000 men were stationed. Barkeley is in west central Texas near Abilene.

Earlier, Ritchie had been accepted to the Army Specialized Training Program to study medicine. The U.S. Army needed doctors. He was to leave Barkeley on December 18 to return to Richmond to attend the Medical College of Viriginia.

However, on December 11, Ritchie was ill with a fever and was placed in the base hospital, an enormous, 200 building complex. For the next several days, his fever continued to be high, though he and the staff were hoping he would get well so he could board a train for Richmond. Nevertheless, he did not improve enough to leave. In fact, he got worse.

The night he was to leave, Ritchie's fever hit 106 degrees, and he was coughing up blood. He died. But he did not know it.

Waking up, Ritchie wondered where he was, looking around his small room for his bag so he could leave. He left the room, walking urgently down halls to find someone to help him. Ritchie spoke loudly to a staff member, who did not even see him.

He went outside, determined to get to Richmond. He began traveling at a high rate of speed, literally flying above the ground, the bushes and tress below, the fields, and towns with lights on. George was amazed. It was not cold or hot.

He was a spirit.

Thought and motion were the same thing. After coming "down to earth," he saw a man outside a store in a town and wanted to ask him where they were. The man did not hear or acknowledge him. George tried to tap his shoulder, but it was like the man was invisible.

George was incredulous. Could it be that these men and the physical objects around him were normal, but that he himself was ... different? What if he made it to Richmond, and no one could see him? What if he was with his family at Christmas, and they could not see him?

A terrible loneliness swept over him. He decided to return to the hospital. So, he began going back, now faster than before. He started to recognize the bushes and trees near the camp. He was at the entrance to the hospital.

Then began one of the strangest searches that can occur: the search for himself. Ritchie knew his small room was somewhere among the 200 barricks, but he had no idea where. He remembers going to get x-rayed, but nothing more. He searched halls and buildings. He saw men in beds but no luck.

Moreover, he had never seen himself for real. That is, he had never seen his 3-D self like others see him. Would he recognize himself? What if he had seen himself already and passed over him?

On and on he searched. Loneliness was now turning to panic. Then he remembered he was wearing his fraternity ring—he would use that as a marker. So he continued to search and search.

He drew back, startled. He found himself, lying with a sheet pulled over his body and head, rigid and unmoving. The body was dead.

Suddenly, the light in the room began to get brighter. The light got brighter and brighter until George realized it was too bright, even dangerous, for physical eyes. It was not a light but a Man.

A Man had entered the room. A man made out of light. The moment he perceived Him, a command formed in his own mind, "Stand up!"[1] The words came from inside him but had authority his own thoughts never had.

He got to his feet and had the certainly that he was in the presence of the Son of God.

The concept of the Son of God had formed inside him, a kind of knowing that immediate and complete. He knew that it was Jesus. George writes: "This Person was power itself, older than time and yet more modern than anyone I had ever met."[2]

For more than power, what emanated from His Presence was unconditional love. Astonishing love. A love beyond his wildest imaging.

Jesus knew everything about George. Along with His radiant presence, every single episode of Ritchie's life was there in full view, taking place at that moment. He cannot explain it.

Time seemed to have ceased. Minutes did not seem to pass. Yet virtually his entire 20 years of existence and all the good and bad memories, including the misery, pain, heartache, the loss of his mother, family quarrels, deep emotional pain, and much, much more, flashed before him.

One question accompanied it all: what did you do with your life?

It was a question about values, not facts. What did you accomplish with the precious time you were allotted?

What have you done with your life to show Me?[3]

George presented some answers. He then realized that the Glory shining around him had no comdemnation. He was not asking about accomplishments or awards. It was about love. How much have you loved with your life? Have you loved others as I am loving you?

They began traveling like George had traveled earlier. They went up in the air, saw a small light below, then descended to the town.

They saw spirit people trying to talk to people on the earth, who could not hear or see the spirit person. They saw a businessman, a woman beggin cigarettes, and a mother, all trying to talk to someone but not even being noticed.

Then they saw a boy trying to talk to his father; a teen boy trailing a teenaged girl through the corridors of a school, and a middle-aged woman begging a gray-haired man to forgive her.

"What are they sorry for, Jesus?" George asked. "Why do they keep talking to people who can't hear them?"

"They are suicides, chained to every consequence of their act."[4]

Then they saw a bar filled with people, drinking liquor. Some of the people were spirit beings, trying to drink but not able to. Some of the beings had a forcefield of light around them, while others did not. After contemplation, Ritchie thought this state of being might be a level of spiritual addiction to some type of behavior on earth.

They moved again. Now they were on the edge of a wide, flat plain, crowded and jammed with hordes of ghostly beings. They were frustrated, angry, miserable beings.

It was a horrific scene. The beings were fighting almost to

the death but not dying. It was like a war without weapons. The creatures were locked in habits of mind and emotion, in hatred, lust, and similar vices. They were engaged in hideous sexual abuses in feverish pantomime.

Yet, no condemnation came from the Presence at George's side, only a compassion for these creatures that breaking His heart.

They moved, and the scene was different. The quality of light was different, more transparent. It was as if Jesus could reveal only what george's mind could grasp.

Now, it was a whole new realm. Almost another existence. George saw enormous buildings in a sunny park. The buildings seemed well-planned.

There was an all-prevading peace. They entered a building, which had high ceilings, tall doorways, and winding staircases. The atmosphere was hushed and still, so Ritchie was startled to see people.

The people were covered with a loose-flowing cloak. He could not tell if they were male or female. The place was like a tremendous study center, humming with the excitement of great discovery.

Everyone they passed seemed to be engrossed in an all-consuming activity, leaving them in total concentration.

They seemed to be absorbed in some vast purpose beyond themselves. In some rooms, these beings were studying intricate charts and diagrams.

George asked Jesus about this place but no explanation was given. The response was one of love and compassion for his ignorance.

They continued on to other buildings in this realm. In one building, music of a complexity and level Ritchie could not comprehend was being created. He thought, Bach is only the beginning!

Another building was a library the size of a university. It was lined with documents floor to ceiling. A phrase kept persisting in his mind: "the key works of the universe."

They visited a hushed and expectant park; a building

crowded with technological machinery; a strange sphere-shaped structure with a walkway over a tank; massive laboratories; a space observatory. Ritchie's mystification grew.

"Is this . . . heaven, Lord Jesus?" asked George.

"When these people were on earth did they grow beyond selfish desires?" he asked Jesus.

They grew, and they have kept on growing. [5]

Up until now, George felt like they were on the earth.

Next, they left the earth behind. They were in an immense void, but it was not frightening. There was a hope and promise in that void.

Then George saw, infinitely far away, something he could never have seen with normal sight . . . a city. It was glowing, bright enough to be seen from such a distance.

The brightness shined from the very walls and even from the beings George could now see moving about the place.

He wondered, could these beings be those who kept Jesus as the focus of their lives . . . and had been changed into His very likeness?

Two beings then detached from the city and started flying toward them at the speed of light. But Jesus and George drew away, even faster. The vision faded. George cried out, but he knew his imperfect sight could not sustain more than a glimpse of this real, ultimate heaven. Jesus had shown him all He could, and now they were speeding away.

The walls of the room appeared. It took George several seconds to realize it. Jesus stood beside him. The glorious city still sparkled and glowed in his thoughts, beckoning and calling him. George saw himself lying in the bed.

Incredibly, Jesus told him he belonged in that form on the bed. George desperately cried out for Jesus not to leave, to make him ready for the shining city, not to leave him in this dark and narrow place.

The Light of Jesus had entered his life and filled it completely, and the idea of being separated from Him was more than he could bear.

The next moment he remembers is opening his eyes with a big headache and seeing a nurse smiling at him.

After he re-entered his body, Ritchie was severely ill for the next several days. In late January, he was discharged and returned to Richmond, Virginia, to attend medical college. He finally got back to Richmond.

FIVE

Kenneth Hagin

KENNETH HAGIN (1917-2003) was a longtime renowned Pentecostal preacher, teacher, writer, and leader, based in Tulsa, Oklahoma, USA. Hagin is the founder of the Word of Faith charismatic movement. There are more than 180 Word of Faith churches in 46 nations.

During his more than 50 years of ministry, his ministry published more than 65 million of his books. Hagin was originally from McKinney, Texas, a suburb of Dallas. His son Kenneth Hagin, Jr., now leads the Word of Faith ministry and the related Rhema Bible Church in Tulsa.

Hagin, Sr., was known for having numerous visions of and experiences with Jesus Christ.

In September, 1950, Hagin experienced one of his more prominent, significant visions, during which he spoke to Jesus, saw the heavenly city, visited the throne of God, received a special anointing, and more. The supernatural experience occurred while Hagin was conducting a tent revival in Dallas suburb of Rockwall.

After giving a lesson during the evening service on September 2, Hagin invited people to come to the front to pray. As he prayed in tongues, he heard a voice say, "Come up hither."[1]

He did not know the voice was speaking to him. Again he heard, "Come up hither." Hagin looked and saw Jesus standing near the top of the tent. The surroundings, such as the tent, chairs, and poles, disappeared, and Hagin saw into the spirit realm.

Jesus was holding a crown in His hands. Hagin writes: "This crown was so extraordinarily beautiful that human language cannot begin to describe it."[2]

Jesus said, "This is a soulwinner's crown. My people are so careless and indifferent. This crown is for every one of My children. I speak and say, 'Go speak to this one or pray for that one,' but My people are too busy. They put it off, and souls are lost because they will not obey Me."[3]

Hagin wept before Him and repented. They then went through the air until they came to a beautiful city. They did not actually go in the city, but they looked at it at close range, just as someone might go up a mountain and look down on a city. The beauty of the city was beyond words.

Jesus said more important things to Hagin and then told him they would go to hell. They left heaven, went toward the earth and went down to hell. Hagin saw human beings wrapped in flames. Hagin had actually visited hell before, on April 22, 1933, when he was 16 years old.

Jesus told him, "Warn men and women about this place."[4]

The Holy Spirit came upon Hagin, and he was under the power of God. He then had one of his major visions. The vision was concerning future events in the United States and the world, prophecy, and end-time events. He also spent more time with Jesus and saw the throne of God. The vision is too extensive to summarize here, but some highlights are below.

Hagin was given scrolls and told to read them. The scroll included such lines and words as "WAR AND DESTRUCTION" and "THE TIME OF THE END OF ALL THINGS IS AT HAND." Jesus told Hagin that the last great revival was taking place. Jesus said, "All the gifts of the Spirit will be in operation in the Church in these last days, and the Church will do greater things than even the Early Church . . ."5

Jesus continued: "Warn this generation, as did Noah his generation, for judgment is about to fall. And these sayings shall be fulfilled shortly, for I am coming soon . . ."6

After reading the scrolls for about 30 minutes, he heard a voice say, "Come up hither! Come up to the throne of God."

Jesus was standing near the top of the tent, and Hagin went to Him through the air. Together, they continued on to heaven. They came to the throne of God, and Kenneth "beheld it in all its splendor. I was not able to look upon the face of God; I only behld His form."7

He saw a beautiful rainbow about the throne. He then noticed the winged creatures on either side of the throne. The creatures had eyes of fire all around their heads, and they looked in all directions at once. When Jesus and Kenneth walked up, the creatures ceased speaking and folded their wings.

As Jesus and Kenneth stood about 20 feet from the throne, Jesus told him not to look upon the face of the One seated on the throne. Kenneth could only see a form of a Being there.

For almost one hour, Jesus spoke to Hagin. Kenneth looked into His eyes, which "looked like wells of living love." Kenneth felt like he could see half a mile deep into Jesus' eyes. He writes: "The tender look of His love is indescribable."8

As Kenneth looked into His face, he fell prostrate at Jesus' feet. Weeping, he laid his palms on the top of Jesus' bare feet and his forehead on his hands. He cried out that he was unworthy to look upon Jesus' face.

Jesus told him to stand upright and called him worthy to look upon His face. Jesus spoke to Kenneth about things concerning his ministry, his calling, about the spiritual warfare surrounding his life and ministry, and similar topics.

Later, Jesus said, "Stretch forth thine hand!" Jesus held out His hands, and Hagin saw the wounds of the crucifixion— "three-cornered, jagged holes . . . large enough for me to put my finger in it."⁹ Jesus laid the finger of His right hand in the palm of Kenneth's right and left hand, and Hagin's hands began to burn as if a hot coal was placed in his hands. Jesus went on to explain to Kenneth about the special anointing for healing the sick He was giving him.

SIX

Betty Malz

As a young woman, Betty Malz experienced heaven in 1959. She died and came back to life eight minutes later.

At the time, Malz was a 27-year-old wife and mother. She was in her hometown of Terre Haute, Indiana, USA. For several weeks, Malz had been experiencing serious, life-threatening health problems and had spent most of that time in the hospital. The problems were the result of a ruptured appendix.

Malz's father was a pastor and devout Christian. Her family, friends, and church family had been praying for her recovery. At the same time, while ill, God was working on Malz's heart regarding certain issues in her life.

Needless to say, her experience was very traumatic as she dealt with severe pain and suffering and was close to death. At times, she was in semi-conscious states, yet she was able to hear medical personnel and friends speak of her imminent passing though the people did not know Malz could hear them.

In the book, Malz also presents several incidents regarding God's intervention in her and her family's circumstances, all part of her story and testimony of God's miraculous plan. After weeks in the hospital, on a cold, winter morning, she actually died at 5:00 a.m.

Malz went through a peaceful transition from the earthly to the heavenly realm. She found herself walking up on a beautiful hill with green grass, the most vivid green she had ever seen. It felt like early spring.

Every blade of grass was about one inch long and with a texture like velvet. The blades were vibrant and moving, and when her feet touched the grass, something alive transmitted up her entire body with every step.

A magnificent blue sky with no clouds was all around her.

An angel walked with her, to her left and a little behind her. Betty felt a special kinship with this angel.

There was no road or path, yet Betty seemed to know exactly where to go. Unlike other hikes, Betty did not get tired at all.

Light was everywhere. Multicolored flowers were blooming. There were trees and shrubs. Somehow, she felt like she was at a high altitude.

Betty had a mixture of emotions, including youth, serenity, fulfillment, health, awareness, and tranquility.

Malz writes: "I felt I had everything I ever wanted to have. I was everything I had ever intended to be. I was arriving at where I had always dreamed of being."[1]

Betty arrived at a wall. Several feet above her head, there was a long row of amber-colored gems. A light from the other side of the wall shone through the precious stones. She thought to herself, "Topaz" (Revelation 21:19-20).* Betty remembered topaz from when she worked at a jewelry store in New Castle, Indiana.

According to Revelation 21:19-20, the heavenly city's walls are adorned with precious stones. Every foundation is listed, with topaz listed ninth. Thus, if every foundation was about a foot high, the topaz level would be about three feet above Betty's head

At the top of a hill, Malz heard her earthly father's voice calling, "Jesus, Jesus, Jesus." Back on earth, her father had prayed those words when he learned that his daughter died.

The voice Betty heard was far away, but she did not turn back because she was going toward a destination.

They walked along in silence for a while. They came upon a magnificent structure. It was like a large palace, silver in color. Betty heard voices proclaiming "Jesus," blending together in a chorus that was melodious and harmonious and in more than four parts. She joined in the singing, realizing that her voice was now what she always wanted it to be like.

The voices began singing a new chorus, now also in a different languages. She was in awe of the richness and perfect blending of the voices. Somehow, she felt like she was part of a universal experience and thus could understand the languages.

Malz sensed that she and the angel could wherever they willed themselves to go. Their communication was through the projection of thoughts.

The angel stepped forward and touched a gate, which was solid pearl and about 12 feet high. It was a Gothic structure. Betty could sense what was going on inside the gate, and it filled her with ecstatic joy and anticipation at the thought of going inside.

At the angel's hand, an opening appeared and slowly grew as if that portion of the gate was being dissolved. Betty saw a golden street covered with either glass or water. A yellow light was dazzling, beautiful beyond description. She knew Jesus was there.

Betty did not move. The light was all around her. She felt heat like she was standing in the sunlight. Her body began to glow. Her being was absorbing the light. Malz: "I felt bathed by the rays of a powerful, penetrating, loving energy."[2]

The angel impressed to Betty: "Would you like to go in and join them?"[3]

She hesitated. She remembered her father's voice. She said she would like to stay and sing a little longer. The gates melted back to being one sheet of pearl. They walked back down the beautiful hill they were on

Then, to her surprise, Betty saw the sun coming up over

the wall. She remembers noticing a shadow from the wall with precious stones.

The worlds of spirit and time and space began to fuse back together. Betty saw Terre Haute, many church steeples, the tops of trees, and then the hospital. She even saw herself on the hospital bed. She descended, slowed down, and stopped.

Betty was back in the hospital. Supernaturally, she saw words stretched out across her room, the letters composed of what looked like translucent, ivory fluid, so alive they pulsated: "I am the resurrection and the life; he that believeth in me, though he were dead, yet shall he live."

Betty sat up in bed. Those around her, including her father, were amazed and dumbfounded at her healing.

SEVEN

Deborah O'Donnell

In 1964, Deborah O'Donnell briefly visited heaven.

Deborah is a wife and mother of four children and a longtime voice and piano teacher in the state of Nebraska, USA. Music has always been a passion for her. From a young girl she has been a Christian.

At the time of her supernatural visit, Deborah and husband Ted were working at their cabin in western Oregon, east of Eugene, Oregon, near the McKenzie River. O'Donnell accidentally inhaled excessive debris from their roof, causing her to fall unconscious in the house.

Deborah realized she was in a place and room she did not recognize. Her surroundings seemed beautiful, beyond what she could imagine. She felt love, joy, and peace. She thought she must be dead.

She walked out of the building and saw people, who did not speak to her. The setting was beautiful.

People were happy and calm. There was a gardener working with the plants. The grass was the greenest and the sky the bluest she had ever seen. O'Donnell walked down a highway that looked like it was made of golden bricks.

Deborah realized that she might get to see her parents.

Even better, she realized she might get to see Jesus. She had no memory of her family on earth.

Suddenly she felt she was being pulled away from where she was, even though she fought with all her might to stay.

She went into the air and looked down at where she was. Her view was like the view from an airplane. She noticed that heaven was like a city. Deborah could see a wall around the city and a massive gate at the entrance. Over the gate she saw the words: "You will return, but I have work for you to do."

EIGHT

Gary Wood

Dr. Gary Wood is a minister, evangelist, and author based in Sugar Land, Texas, USA, a suburb of Houston.

Wood, his wife Deena, and their team minister around the world. Gary has written books, recorded a CD, and regularly appears on national television and radio programs. Among his many ministries, Gary oversees churches and ministers to Navajo Indians in New Mexico. Wood has a Doctorate in Theology from Grace Theological Seminary.

A lifelong Christian, Wood experienced heaven after a serious car wreck. Gary was 18 years old when the accident and his visit to heaven occurred.

On the night of December 23, 1966, Gary and his sister Sue were driving in their hometown of Farmington, New Mexico, USA. In the darkness, a tow truck was illegally parked in Gary and Sue's lane. There was no time to react, and they hit the truck. Gary died.

Though he felt sharp pain when the wreck took place, Gary quickly felt peace and no pain. He rose up into a funnel-shaped cloud and then began to walk on a moving pathway similar to airport walkways. A brilliant light engulfed him. He knew he was going north.

The funnel opened up wide, then Gary saw what looked like a giant golden satellite, high in the air, suspended in heaven. Approaching heaven, an angel with a sword allowed him in.

Wood stood on a hill, on lush green grass. When he started walking, the grass came through his feet.

Beautiful singing surrounded him. Having earned a music degree in school, Wood had great appreciation for the singing he heard. The songs of angels were "overwhelming, beyond what I can capture in mortal words."[1]

Wood believes that heaven is 1,500 miles in every direction, and 780,000 stories high. He saw the 12 foundational stones of the city, layered on top of each other. The stones were jasper (diamonds), sapphires, sardis, beryl, topaz, emeralds, rubies, and so forth. He saw the 12 gates, one for each tribe of Israel. Each gate was made of one single pearl.

A loved one is assigned to show someone around heaven. Gary's friend John, who had passed away in high school, met Gary to escort him. They hugged and "went into one another," literally.

They first went to a room similar to a library, lined with solid gold walls. Angels took care of the room. They were all at least 40 feet tall and had different features, such as very strong and muscular, long hair, and so forth.

The many books recorded earthly histories and salvations.

Wood was able to see a man on earth receive Jesus as Lord and Savior. When this event was reported in the recording room in heaven, an angel took that man's book and wiped out all his transgressions he had committed up until that time. An angel opened the Lamb's Book of Life and wrote his name in it.

Gary saw sins literally erased out of books. He also saw his own book. He saw records of spiritual growth and how people respond to certain situations. He even saw a set of books which has record of every person's name and their every thought, intent, and everything they do from birth on. Wood believes that anyone who does not receive Jesus Christ will be judged out of those books on the Great White Throne of Judgment.

Gary saw people sitting on bleachers watching people on earth being saved (Hebrews 12:1).

He saw angels carrying bowls into the presence God, bowls with the praises of God's people on earth and in heaven.

The angels present the bowls at the throne of God. The throne is "all light, surrounded by a great aura of indescribable colors."

The angels disappeared into a thick mist. They also carried bowls of water-like liquid, which are the tears of the saints on earth.

Lightning and thunder came from the throne, but there was no fear or scaryness.

Gary saw seven golden lamps of fire, representing the Holy Spirit.

He saw a glorious crystal clear body of water flowing from the throne.

The rainbows of colors around the throne were intense.

When Gary saw Jesus, he was overwhelmed and fell down like a dead man. Jesus picked him up.

Jesus had a radiant, beautiful light coming from Him. His voice was like the water flowing over massive waterfalls.

He wore a crown and a regal robe of righteousness that was pure white, with a purple sash. He had a solid gold belt around his waist. He was about six feet two inches tall with an olive complexion.

Wood: "His eyes were deep, beautiful pools of love."[2] When He looked at Gary, His eyes pierced him with pure love, going all the way through him. Gary melted.

Gary could see the indentions on His brow from the

crown of thorns. Gary could see where the nails had been driven into his wrists (not His palms) and where one nail had been driven through both feet as they were crossed.

Jesus said to him: "Tell My people there's a song for them to sing, a message to proclaim, a missionary jouney to take, a book to write. They all have a purpose for being here in this life. Don't ever believe the condemnation of the devil that you are unworthy. You are worthy. You have been redeemed by the blood of the Lamb. Why do My people not believe in Me? Why do My people reject Me?"[3]

Gary fell down again. Jesus picked him up again. The words were burned into his spirit and the walls of his soul. Jesus asked again, "Why do they not walk in My commandments?"

Jesus commissioned Wood to make Him real to people on earth. Jesus spoke, "Tell people they are special and unique, each one. God made every one of His children to have a divine purpose, which only they can accomplish on earth."[4]

Gary went to his own mansion. It was not finished. There were three buckets of paint in the living room. John and Gary threw paint on the wall, and suddenly flowers appeared everywhere along with a sweet floral aroma.

Wood noticed three different types of clothing in heaven:
1. Everyday clothing—soft and velvety; tapers to the body
2. Robe of salvation—fits on top of everyday clothing; linen
3. Robe of righteousness—worn on top of robe of salvation; sleeveless; worn in the presence of God, in the throne room (Isaiah 61:10); also called a "garment of praise" (Isaiah 61:3); decorated with all kinds of jewels and decorations indicating what you did on earth.

Then, Gary saw a river of life coming directly from the throne room of God. John gave Gary a robe, and they stepped in the water. Gary could breathe in the water and interact with it. Wood: "It vitalized me, invigorated me, and gave me strength. I drank some of the water—it was so very refreshing, sweet, and rejuvenating."[5]

Gary then stood on the river bank and saw a group singing a well-known worship song on earth. He asked John about the song, and John explained that all songs of the spirit originate in heaven. Gary saw musical notes floating in the air and going "into" a person who would begin to sing in the spirit.

The angels sang along with the group's singing, and even the trees clapped and kept rhythm. The flowers had faces and sang along as well. Gary was astounded.

Walking along, Gary noticed that the streets of gold were transparent. He saw angels sculpting clay. John explained the angels were forming miscarried babies into what "God wants them to be." He saw a child run into the arms of Jesus, who Gary noticed spent much of His time with children and teens.

Near the throne room, about 500 yards away, they saw a storage room called "Unclaimed Blessings." Gary was amazed to see every part of the anatomy stored in the room. He saw legs hanging from the walls. In short, God has miracles waiting to give to people.

Gary saw people on earth pray and the prayers go to heaven. The angels received the prayers and got the specific miracle needed (a body part, an organ, etc.) Gary noticed that the enemy hinders the prayers and discourages people; angels often had to fight principalities and powers. The people would give up, thinking they would never receive the miracle.

This revelation confirms the importance of faith and persistence in prayer.

Gary's sister on earth was praying for Gary's life. John told Gary that the latter would have to go back to earth, because his sister is using the Name.

The next moment, Gary was "catapulted back into [his] body."[6]

Wood had actually been dead for 20 minutes. He was brain dead. Doctors said Gary would never be able to talk again.

But a few days after returning to his body, Jesus appeared in his hospital room and healed Dr. Gary Wood.

NINE

Richard Eby

Dr. Richard Eby (1912-2003) was a nationally recognized osteopathic physician and had a distinguished medical career in California, USA.

Eby was the co-founder of Park Avenue Hospital in Pomona, California, where he practiced medicine for many years. He was also one of the original founders of what became Western University of Health Sciences in Pomona. Today, Western U has more than 3,700 students and 2,000 staff people and an additional location in Eugene, Oregon. Western's website is WesternU.edu.

In 1972, at the age of 60, Richard had a near-death experience and visited heaven. After his supernatural visit, his career path took a turn as he dedicated himself to the work of evangelism. Eby and his wife Maybelle had two children and five grandchildren.

Five years later, Jesus appeared to him in human form and allowed him to experience hell.

Eby was a devout Christian throughout his youth and adult life. His medical, scientific background and perspective impacts his testimony of his time in heaven. Eby's reports about heaven are permeated with a medical professional's objective, inquisitive analysis, detailed descriptions, and fascinating insight.

An accident preceded his heavenly visit. On a hot summer day in 1960, Eby was working at a relative's home in Chicago, Illinois, USA, helping pack and throw boxes from the house's second and third story to the ground below. After a broken railing gave way, Eby fell from the house, landing on the cement below. He was immediately unconscious and experienced heaven.

His tragic fall onto the sidewalk was devastating and very scary for his wife Maybelle who was there that day. In short, Richard died. He had no pulse and was not breathing when the ambulance arrived. Nevertheless, Maybelle prayed and believed for a miracle, and a neighbor immediately began a prayer chain at a local church.

Maybelle and those praying had no idea that Eby was in heaven, a visit he calls "unutterable . . . indescribable . . . spiritually resplendent . . . and most ecstatically moving."[1]

Richard landed in heaven, not on a cloud but on solid ground and with joyous excitement.

Instantly, he was in another world. He cannot adequately describe the astonishment, the amazement, and the sheer shock of this event.

Eby went from the miserable humidity of Chicago to the most exquisite place prepared for followers of Jesus.

The first thing he noticed was an indescribable sense of peace that passes all understanding, joy, comfort, and release. He felt at home. Moreover, he felt God at his very core. It all happened so fast.

Noticing his surroundings, Richard's sight was fixed on the exquisite valley he was in. The scene was "gorgeously unsurpassable in its beauty," with the foliage having a radiance. It was a great outdoors of mountains, trees, flowers, music, and sweet smells.

There was not a shadow anywhere, and he sensed God's presence everywhere.[2]

Forests of symmetrical trees unlike anything on earth covered the foothills on each side. Every tree was tall, graceful, perfect, unblemished and were a duplicate of the others. The trees resembled evergreen, arbor vitae trees but were entirely unique. Every leaf and branch was perfect. Richard wondered why the trees and flowers were identical. The answer was immediate: in heaven, creation has remained perfect, and things grow alike.

Rolling hills under cloudless skies seemed to stretch for miles. The skies were a new color, an iridescent white-gold light.

The valley floor was gorgeous. Stately grasses with perfectly straight blades were mixed in with ultra-white, four-petalled flowers on stems two feet tall, with a touch of gold at the centers. Every one of them was identical.

Eby decided to pick a bouquet, and they were already in his hand! Amazingly, his thought became his act. He realized there was no time lag in Paradise. A word spoken or thought became fact.

The flower was of liquid gold and transparent through to the stem. The stems were vibrantly alive and soft as silk but had no moisture. As a doctor, Eby was inquisitive about the internal workings of his surroundings. He wondered how the flowers could live without water.

The Lord replied that on earth, there is temporary life support from hydrogen and oxygen, which are not needed in heaven, because living water flows from the throne of God.[3] Gasping while examining the flowers, Eby wondered how the flowers were so white. Instantly the answer came: on earth, white light mixed with the light of the sun. In heaven, Jesus the Light of the World provides the perfect light. In Him all things exist and have their being.[4]

Richard looked down to see what he had landed on: firm ground with plants, green grass, flowers, and trees. Each growing thing emitted its own light in the appropriate color.

Everything in heaven seemed to produce its own light. Eby was given the scripture "the heavens declare the glory of God."[5]

Mind

Richard's new mind was completely captivating. He went from having a flesh-restricted mind to a heaven-released mind which functioned at the speed of light![6]

His mind seemed to have become part of God's mind.

To Eby, it was an indescribable experience. He realized that with his liberated mind, "response to each thought would be a simultaneous answer or act. Before I could compose or complete a thought or wish, the answer was given or the requested action was occurring."[7] Richard realized he was sharing the Mind of Christ, almost like borrowing His omniscience to do his own thinking (see 1 Corinthians 2).

Totally enveloped in God's presence, Eby realized that God was with him, in him, and surrounding him (see John 17: 21-23, 26).

Body

Richard was absolutely astounded and amazed at his new, "exquisitely different" body. In childlike glee, he inspected it and noticed supernatural facets of this heavenly body.

He realized he was the same size and shape he was on earth—yet this body was totally different. The "material" of it was unknown to him: cloudlike, gorgeously self-illuminated, and transparent to the direct gaze, with no bones, organs, or blood (see 1 Cor. 15: 50). His abdomen and chest were organless and transparent to his gaze, though they emitted light to his peripheral vision.[8]

His mind worked with electric-like speed and answered his unspoken question: none of these bodily functions were needed, because Jesus is the Life in heaven.[9]

In his new body, Richard felt like a child and could feel the sense of timelessness like a sixth sense. He was totally overwhelmed with the sense of joy, peace, comfort, and freedom as well as the beauty.[10]

He had no memory of earth and no pain and enjoyed his heavenly body.

His clothing was a translucent flowing white gown,

transparent to his gaze, made of rare fabric that was silk-like yet firm (see Revelation 19:8).[11]

In amazement, he could see through his body and see the gorgeous white flowers beneath him. It seemed perfectly normal yet thrillingly novel. He could walk "through" grass, flowers, and even trees; grass and flowers simply snapped back to their perfect state.

The whole time, he was instinctively aware that the Lord of Lords was everywhere. The sense of timelessness made all hurry foolish. He sensed he was in an anteroom to heaven.

Being a doctor, he noticed certain physical and physiological qualities of his body. His range of vision was unlimited, sharp, and clear, no matter the distance. Ten miles seemed like 10 inches.[12]

Richard realized that he was the same person in heaven as he was on earth, albeit without the physical compenents. While on earth, he had often been more concerned with the outer container of his body rather than the "contents."

Noticing his spirit person, he again asked a question: why is there no death in heaven? Again there was an instant answer: organs die, while the spirit is eternal. God made the spirit man in His own image.

All in all, Eby notes what a beautiful, perfect, self-illuminated, weightless body he had. Moreover, he was genderless. He quickly asked why. The answer: "I never told mankind to repopulate heaven—only earth. Up here there is no marriage. Everyone here is created or reborn" (see Matthew 22:30 and Genesis 1:28).[13]

Sounds

Eby was overwhelmed.

The whole time he was in heaven, Richard was aware of beautiful, angelic background music, which seemed to fit unobstrusively into the whole experience.

He listened closely and noticed it was beautifully different from anything on earth. It was beyond instrumental or vocal, so beautiful that no earthly adjectives could describe it.[14]

Eby quickly discovered why it was different: it had no beat, and it came from everywhere.

As Eby started to ask God why there was no beat, he already had the answer. Eternity is a place where timelessness cannot be divided up into beats.

Richard asked where the music was coming from. God reminded Eby about the law of physics, referring to the law of resonance, in which two objects of similar material, density, and tension vibrate in unity when one is activated. God explained that He created heaven and everything in it, and it all vibrates with Him. He is the Composer and has given heaven this new song.

Amazingly, fascinatingly, Eby noticed that even his clothing was singing softly, as was his body, the flowers, trees, hills, and sky (see 1 Chronicles 16:31-33).[15]

Smells

To his surprise, perhaps the sweetest revelation was the aroma of heaven. It was everywhere, bathing his being. He closed his eyes to enjoy the exquisite smells.

This time, Richard did not receive an answer to his internal query about the fragrance. When he was back on earth, the Lord advised him to search the scriptures. There, Eby noticed that throughout the Bible, God reveals His love of sweet-smelling aromas, including: the aroma related to sacrifices of His people; incense in Tabernacle worship; his joy from the prayers of the saints; and more (see also Revelation 5:8).

During this divine transmitting of God's thoughts to Eby's mind and spirit, Richard was realizing how much there was to learn about reigning with God throughout eternity.

Richard wanted to find his wife, so he instantly went down a straight path. Hearing her distant voice calling him, the valley grew dim and then went out.[16]

The next day, Jesus visited and spoke to Eby in the hospital room:

"Suddenly the room lit up. I moved my eyes toward the source: out of the plaster where the ceiling met the walls was emerging the most gorgeously sculptured cloud of "milk-glass" texture , self-illuminated! ... The Cloud was smoothly formed of rounded billows, four feet long and half as wide. "It" detached from the plaster and hung beautifully in space. Then it spoke! And the voice was Jesus! Sovereign, regal, loving, authoritative, sweet, winsome, meek, powerful! All rolled in one...He said:

"My peace I give unto you!"

"With your hands you will heal."...

I looked up again, and he repeated his promise: "My peace I give unto you! With your hands you will heal."[17]

Five years later, in 1977, Eby was on a tour in Israel when Jesus appeared to him and gave him a divine message. Richard was actually in the famous tomb of Lazarus when the miraculous encounter and experience happened.

First, Richard felt a man next to him. Then he saw the toes protruding from the flowing robe, then the golden sash, beautifully muscled arms, and shoulder-length, light golden hair.

Richard is not able to describe the royalty of Jesus' face—its sovereignty, compassion, and overwhelming look of righteousness. Eby: "In it I saw the justice of our intercessor, the joy of our healer, the humility of his father's faithful servant. I saw a display of meekness without weakness, of limitless power with infinite gentleness and those penetrating eyes, emitting a radiance of indescribably limitless love! Nothing can be compared with the eyes of our God. They held me spellbound."

Jesus spoke to Richard, just as He had when they were in heaven: "My son! I must show you hell, but just for two minutes! I have already shown you heaven. I want you to tell them, tell them, tell them."

As though in shock, I stood stock-still, wondering what I should 'tell them'. He already knew my thoughts and was answering me at a million words a second. I will try to summarize his command to me.

> "You must tell them that I gave them a will when I created them. They must make a choice between me and my adversary, Satan. Man cannot live without a master; his soul is made to worship someone. Tell them I am a gentleman; I will never override their free will. I created them to be free to choose, because I would not create anyone to be a slave. Satan offers them the security of slavery, but his wages are death. I offer them freedom and the righteousness of My Father in heaven, where our gift of love and life is eternal."

In seconds, Jesus had transmitted to me volumes of spiritual data, bypassing my ears and brain which would have been far too sluggish to receive his instructions. For emphasis he repeated insistently:

> "Tell them. Tell them. Tell them. Tell them how much I love them! I left heaven to come and die for them. I had to destroy the works of the devil so my children could be freed! I arose to present them blameless before my Father in heaven! Tell them they can choose life with Me--all for free. I paid the price. Tell them they will have the unsearchable riches that my Father has prepared for them. They can choose to belong to the family of God. They can reign with me as kings and priests through the ages. I will send them my spirit. I will heal their infirmities. I will forgive their sins. Tell them I took their place on my cross!"

At this Eby shuddered.

"Tell them, my grace is sufficient for them. It is my gift of live. They cannot earn it by their works. I finished all the work and waiting on the cross. All they must do is receive me into their hearts and accept me as their Way of Life. Then we will be one!'

He suddenly paused, and I noted a tone of sorrow (perhaps horror) as he spoke again:

"Tell them if they ignore or reject my love, if they turn away from my Father, if they refuse to listen to the urgings of the spirit, there is nothing more that we can do fo them. They remain under the control of Satan, that liar and deceiver, for whom I had to create hell when he defied the Almighty God. Because Jehovah is righteous, we had to punish Satan's wickedness and rebellion. I never intended a human soul to go to hell; in fact I came down from heaven and died for mankind to redeem him from that deceiver. I even went to hell and took the keys. I sealed Satan's fate, and secured victory over hell and death. Tell them, my name is above all names, but they must choose whom they will serve!"

Then his voice changed. Like a trumpet it echoed about the tomb: "There is yet a little while- but very little!"[18]

Suddenly, Eby was in hell. Instantly, knowing he was trapped, he found himself in a stone, coffinlike cell, four feet wide and six a half feet high. The terror was instantaneous and indescribable.

He tried to scream but had no voice. There was total blackness and total stench, surely from demons. Sure enough, he looked down and saw clearly many little, spiderlike demons about his feet. Among them were several deformed catlike and doglike creatures with black feces-matted fur. They were in constant movement, and each one fastened its gaze upon him as the smaller ones swarmed up the walls beside his face. Flames were behind each eye. The stench was nauseating.

The 'chained demons' spoke: 'We are the chained demons, here to haunt and taunt you in hell!'

Richard was snatched upward and back to Lazarus' tomb, with the light on. His two minutes in hell without Jesus had ended.[19]

Since the visit, Jesus has told him to "Tell them, tell them, tell them," so Eby did, through his talks, messages, books and much more.[20]

TEN

Rhoda "Jubilee" Mitchell

RHODA "JUBILEE" MITCHELL is an evangelist, author, civil servant, and mother in Illinois, USA. In 1974, at age 25, she visited heaven.

Now retired, Mitchell worked previously in a civilian capacity as a Civil Servant for the U.S. Air Force. She is a mother of two children with a large extended family. From a young age, Jubilee received prophetic dreams and visions.

At that time of her heavenly visit, things were not going well for Mitchell. She was depressed and overwhelmed. Prostrate on the floor, face down, she cried out to God, pleading with Him.

Suddenly Jesus appeared next to her. She saw herself lying face down. All at once, Jesus and Jubilee were flying up into the sky. She could see through the house below her. Her senses were heightened.

Her mind was alert and refreshed. She felt more alive than ever before. She could see through and even go through walls.

As they ascended, the night sky was dark and filled with stars. The view was breathtaking. Jubilee remembers that the moon was to the upper left of them. She was in Jesus' arms, resting in peace.[1]

Amazingly, she was aware of Jesus communicating with the Father.

Jubilee was in awe at the unfolding of the heavens, with its sparkling stars and shining planets, all declaring the love of God. God's love "began shooting through [her] like arrows aimed directly at [her] heart."[2] His love consumed her.

When her spirit was separated from her body, Mitchell began receiving revelations and impartations. All the questions she ever had were answered. Mitchell: "Imagine having all of your questions answered in an instant."[3] It was exhilarating.

Jubilee was amazed that God could be so big and powerful yet still be very concerned about her own feelings.

Before them, she saw a brilliant scene: a star shining in the dark void. It looked like the sun: beautiful, white, yellowish, and floating. Jubilee realized that God's creation praises and adores Him; and that God's presence generates the creation process. Wherever He is, new life is born.

Jubilee was amazed at the sights and experiences in deep space, as she and Jesus flew at an incredibly fast speed through the heavens. Yet she was completely at peace and loved by Jesus.

They flew past a star that was exploding, with blinding white light shooting in every direction. She was surprised by all the colors in space: electric blues, yellow, and deep pinks. The lights shot and refracted through space like a science fiction movie.[4]

The Spirit of Father God filled the space they flew through.

The brilliant star before them got bigger and bigger, until it was right before them, like a planet. Heaven. They arrived.

Jesus informed Jubilee that she was only there for a visit.

They flew over the walls and landed inside. Jesus set her down on a small, grassy hill. He told her that only people who have died can enter by the gates.

Her sense of peace was indescribable. She was fully

happy. Angels in white robes gave her a tour. She saw angels of different kinds. The cherubim had two wings, while the seraphim had six wings.

There were also creatures, almost like beasts that were not frightening. Some of them were part human and part animal. One had a muscular male human body and the face of a lion. She saw creatures with the body of a lion and the head of an eagle.[5]

Jubilee saw a yellowish, perfect jewel about one foot by six inches, embedded in a section of the wall. She looked through it, realizing it was a window to the city. These jewels were different sizes, including large ones. They looked like a master jeweler had made them.

The light from the city shined through the jewel windows, becoming rainbow light shows with bright, kaleidoscopic, multi-colored rays.

Her guided tour continued. Jubilee saw mountains, hills, and countryside. The street through the middle of the city was perfectly straight, with intersecting streets that formed right angles with the main street.[6]

The streets glowed. She looked at her feet, which seemed to be several inches of water. The street looked transparent, like it had water on it, but it was solid.

Jubilee came to a charming area with simple and elegant homes, almost like adobes. The setting looked like a small Spanish town. There was a fountain with water spouting up in perfection.

There were all types, nationalities, and ages of people in the city.

Jubilee saw and spent time with young people. There were babies who died as infants as well as aborted babies. The children were "full of fun" and very inquisitive like all children, but they were also very knowledgable and insightful. Jubilee met six-year-olds with strong intellect who wanted to sit in her lap.

In another section of the city, there was a block party with many in attendance. All the rejoicing, dancing, and singing was directed toward the Lord. People wore beautiful, sparkling, colorful clothing and dazzling, white robes. The people were happy and were twirling, jumping, and praising God.

Jubilee learned that in heaven, there are infinite ways to praise the Lord. When someone offered a song or poem of praise, the city became very quiet and then erupted with excitement as everyone joined in praise together. People might sculpt a great work of art, paint a lovely picture or something similar, in worship and praise of God. The music in heaven was spectacular and had great diversity.

While people sang and talked verbally, often communication was non-verbal. Mitchell experienced the same in her communication with the Father and Jesus: sometimes verbal, sometimes "telepathically," or non-verbal.

She even discusses that sometimes in heaven, she could hear other's thoughts if they were close in proximity.

Heaven was beyond Jubilee's imagination. It was a place of purpose, righteousness, and beauty. While some may think heaven will be a "dreamy-like" state, Jubilee reports "it is just the opposite—it is the ultimate reality."[7]

As she walked through the city, she saw Jesus walking along a street parallel to where she was. Jesus was with a group of people and angels.

A sphere of glorious light surrounded Jesus. His countenance glowed like the sun, but brighter. The light around Jesus was the whitest, brightest light imaginable, like an electric splendor, about four feet in diameter. It was pure white. It was like the sun was moving with him. The light was the glory and anointing of God.

Another time, Mitchell thought she saw the sun rising above a hill. It was actually Jesus walking toward her. Then He told her things to share with people: that He wants us to get close to Him, to share His anointing, to walk with Him in the fire of His glory. He wants to pull us into His presence.[8]

Jubilee gained an entirely new perspective on the concept

of "kingdom living." She realized that Jesus is the King of kings and that we are kings and His royal subjects. In heaven, there is pageantry and ceremonies. Some people receive soul winner's crowns. The crowns actually had bits of real celestial stars in them, sparkling and shining with the brightest of light. The crowns and the stars gave off dazzling rays of light.[9]

Again and again, Jubilee was in awe of the sights and sounds of heaven. For example, the choirs' music was captivating. Some choirs were people, some were angels, and some were both people and angels.

Jesus took Jubilee over the walls of the city and into their descent. She felt like she was falling a far distance at a tremendous speed. As she went down, the freedom of heaven waned. The glory of heaven was going away. She could see the roof of her home and her body lying on the bed. When her spirit went back into her body, she felt a jolting sensation and took a deep breath, feeling like she had just awakened from a deep sleep.

ELEVEN

Valvita Jones

In 1974, Valvita Jones, 25, was in the hospital with serious health problems. She was being treated at Kansas University Medical Center, USA, for infections, which turned into a very serious crisis causing her and the medical team to fight for her life.

A feeling of peace came over her, and she started to move upward. She was above the hospital room and vaguely remembers seeing the team working on her.

She felt like she passed through three heavens. In the first heaven, Jesus Christ met her and led her through the heavens.

Jesus physical presence faded away, as Valvita was caught up in his love. She looked into his eyes, which were loving and clear as blue water, yet piercing. It was like she was mirrored in his eyes. Jesus looked straight through and into her. Valvita know right away that he knew everything about her.

There was a heavenly illumination that made his hair light red, his eyes bluish and transparent, and his skin a light gold color. Jones writes: "There is no way to describe his coloring. It is like another world's color. It's the Shekinah glory, iridescent golden light glowing through him. In his resurrection body, his coloring is uniquely different from anything on earth."[1]

In Jones' experience, the first heaven was a brilliant light blue. In an instant, it opened up and split down the middle, with both sides rolling back like scrolls. The second two skylike heavens rolled back like scrolls as well.

In just a few seconds, Jones was in the presence of the Most High, God the Father. She felt an awesome glory, and she realized He was on the throne.

The throne was massive. Valvita felt like it extended all the way earth, and that earth was part of the throne. She fell prostrate to the ground.

God spoke to her, and the Father's communication sounded like many waters rushing. She lied there a long time. Much of the communication with God was about Jones' life and how she interacted with people, realizing there were ways she could have done things better as well as situations she handled well. She felt completely unworthy.

Then Jesus touched her with his hand, and her strength returned. He led her to the side of an arena. She writes: "He looked into my eyes, into my soul, and I knew he knew and understood everything I felt. When he looked into me, it was with more love than I ever thought possible for anyone to know."[2]

Jesus stepped away from Valvita and went alone into the light. The Father's light and Jesus' light blended together. As Jones puts it, "They both gave off light and their light was the same light. I will never forget this as long as I live."[3]

When Jesus stepped away from Jones, He turned sideways and stretched out His arms like a bridge. One arm extended to Valvita and one to the Father. Jones believes Jesus was making a visual representation of a bridge and of the verses 1 Timothy 2:5-6.

Valvita heard the Father and Jesus communing about her case. Jesus said, "My blood is sufficient. She's mine."[4] Jones celebrated. Then Jesus returned to her, and they celebrated together, after which Jesus continued teaching her.

He also told her that she would have to go back to earth, "Yes, because there is a work I have for you to do."[5]
Valvita returned to her body as what felt like the speed of light.

TWELVE

Roberts Liardon

ROBERTS LIARDON IS a nationally acclaimed minister, teacher, author, and Christian leader. He has built churches, founded Bible colleges, ministered in more than 100 nations, and authored more than 40 books.

In 1974, at the age of eight, Liardon was taken to heaven. While there, Jesus took him on a tour, taught him, and spent considerable time with him.

Jesus escorted Roberts to the following places: streets of gold, a family's home, the River of Life, a large building holding a service of praise, storehouses of heaven, and the building that is the Throne Room of God. Along the way, Jesus spoke to Liardon and passed on many truths.

At the time, Roberts was living in Tulsa, Oklahoma, USA, with his mother, grandmother, and sister Priscilla. The Liardon home was a disciplined, Christian place, with much prayer and Bible study. Roberts' grandmother and grandfather had been Pentecostal pastors and church planters.

The visit to heaven was a complete surprise to young Roberts. It was summertime, and he came inside the house to his room to do his daily Bible reading. One of his and his sister's daily chores was to read four chapters of the Bible every day, so that they would read the entire Bible in one year.

He sat down on the bed, laid back, and placed his head on a pillow, with a children's Bible on his chest. Suddenly, without warning, his room and even his body disappeared. He felt a presence and an energy, which he knows now was the anointing and presence of God.

Roberts felt himself being pulled through the roof at a high rate of speed. As he rose up, he saw the oceans far away and then the lights in the heavens. In hindsight, he now knows he was traveling through the first and second heavens on his way to the third heaven (2 Corinthians 12:2).

In seconds, Liardon landed on a flat space about the size of a living room floor, outside of a massive gate. It was tall, wide, and perfect, without a cut or blemish. The gate was one solid, immense, glossy, glowing pearl, with a carved design on the edges. The gate had a literal presence, like a glow.

It all happened very fast. Roberts shook himself to see if he was dreaming. Then he touched the gate and heard, "This is one of the gates."[1]

As he turned around, he saw Jesus Christ. Roberts recognized Him immediately. The glory about Him moved toward Roberts and came upon him, engulfing him. Roberts fell to his knees, and tears began to stream from his eyes, running down his face. The presence of Jesus brought out the tears, not a human emotion like sadness or excitement.

Jesus said, "I want to give you a tour through heaven, this place I have made for all who believe, because I love you so much."[2]

As he said this, tears again poured down Roberts' face. To Roberts, Jesus' presence is so tender that your joy turns to tears.

Then Jesus said, "Now, no more tears, but a face full of joy would make me glad," and He laughed, and Roberts did also.[3]

Many people ask Liardon what Jesus looked like. Roberts points out that when you see Jesus, you are so overwhelmed by His presence that His appearance is secondary. Yet Liardon does describe Him.

Jesus was the "perfect man ... The way He looked, talked, and moved seemed the epitome of perfection and wholeness." He was around 5'11" to 6'1" tall, muscular, with olive-toned skin, a beard, and hair that came almost to his shoulders.[4]

From Roberts' experience, "every time Jesus speaks, it is as if arrows of faith propelled by love shoot into you and explode inside. Your only way of reacting is to weep."[5]

The Lord walked to Roberts, picked him up, and dried his face.

He escorted Roberts through the massive gate. The gate simply opened for Jesus, and they walked through.

The first thing Roberts saw was a street made of gold. As he walked on, all the streets looked like they were pure gold. Some of the gold looked like earthly gold, while some of it was transparent and as clear as crystal.

Realizing he should not stand on gold, Roberts raced to the curb. Jesus continued to walk ahead and turned to tell Roberts something. Looking over at Liardon, Jesus asked, "What are you doing over there?"

Roberts explained himself in just two words, "Golden streets!" Jesus laughed and laughed, with a deep laugh from within. Then he told Roberts, "Come over here."[6]

Trying to explain that he couldn't walk on gold, as it was so valuable, Jesus continued to beckon him, "Come on," as he continued laughing, walking over to where Roberts was and leading him back onto the street.

Along the curbs, the grass was so green Liardon cannot explain it. It was the "original essence and very fullness" of green. All colors in heaven are so vibrant they make earthly colors seem faded.[7]

Flowers in all the colors of the rainbow lined the curbs. The flowers hummed with life, like a vibration and surge from the life of God that fills heaven.

Roberts noticed that there was a light, free, and joyful atmosphere in heaven, with no sense of hurry.

Moreover, the fruit of the Holy Spirit energizes heaven. The actual breezes are filled with the presence of God.

They walked on, passing towns, buildings, and small offices. Roberts saw people coming and going, smiling and happy. Some sang songs. Many carried small bundles of items, such as books. He saw a woman go into a place with a bundle of goods and leave with a book.

Liardon believes there are books and songs in heaven that are meant for people on earth. Men and women must pay the price to bring them to the earth.

In a small town, they turned right on a street and then walked up an unpaved path. Up ahead, Roberts saw a gigantic house above the trees. In heaven, he saw different kinds of mansions and homes, with each one seeming to fit the desires of the person who dwells there. The homes have touches of both heaven and earth.

During their walk up the path, Jesus talked to Roberts the whole time, like a friend.

When they arrived at the door of the house, Jesus knocked. They waited about three minutes, and then Jesus knocked again. Then, a man opened the door and greeted them both by name. Roberts was amazed that everyone they met in heaven knew his name and knew he was a visitor.

Conversations were just like they are on earth. The man asked how they were doing and invited them inside. They walked into a living room or den area. The furniture was so comfortable it snuggled up to Roberts.

Jesus and the man spoke about revival. Those in heaven have knowledge of events on earth, mainly concerning the movements of God and of humans.

After talking, the man took them through the house, which was in Roberts' view, total perfection. There were many rooms, windows, art on the walls, beautiful furniture, luxuries, photographs of the man's family members, and many plants. In addition, there were things Roberts did not recognize.

The man gave Roberts a large fruit to eat, similar to an

apple, which was delicious. They said goodbye and walked out the back door. The other people in the house hugged and kissed them before they left.

The people in heaven looked in perfect condition and in the prime of life, perhaps in their 30s. People were polite and friendly.

Toward Jesus, people were reverent, but also comfortable and natural.

The people wore white robes which seemed to radiate from within. Some had sashes, and some had jewelry.

As they crossed some hills, Roberts saw all kinds of animals, including a dog, a baby goat, and a lion of great strength. The animals were calm and peaceful, like everything else. He saw birds singing in the trees, even singing the same song. When they stopped, they seemed to be talking to each other.

The leaves of the trees swayed back and forth, dancing and praising, like a wind was blowing through.

The goodness of God abounds in heaven.

Jesus and Roberts became friends as the Lord gave him a tour of heaven.

Also, Roberts received a revelation about peoples' age in heaven. He believes that when people get to heaven, they will be their spiritual age; that is, the age they are in the hidden man, based on their spiritual maturity. They will not be their age of physical maturity.

Roberts saw many angels, who were tall and strong. They were about six to eight feet tall and dressed according to their position.

Some have wings, which make a musical sound when they move. There are many types of angels.

In the presence of Jesus, the angels were almost silent, resepctful, and reserved.[8]

They soon came to a massive building, similar to a convention center on earth. The building had a glowing circle around it. Thousands of people were streaming inside.

Two angels met them and escorted them down to the

second row, where there were two seats reserved. On the way, people greeted them. It was like a family reunion, with people hugging and kissing each other and saying, "How are you? Glory to God!" Love was everywhere.

As soon as they were seated, a holy silence filled the place. A choir of 500 to 600 praisers entered, smiling, dressed like a church choir on earth. When they started singing, the place erupted. Everyone lifted their hands and danced, leaping up and down in dance. Praise services on earth do not compare. The service lasted about two hours.

Everyone moved in unison, with no one person leading. Everything was done in perfect order. Jesus was smiling and enjoying the service. Suddenly, the praise ended abruptly.

The praise was like bright, glowing vapors that collected at the top of the building. When the service was over, the collected praise shot out of the building and went to the throne room of God. Roberts realized that praise is a substance.

Liardon believes that when everyone gives their all and 100 percent in worship, supernatural things occur, such as miracles. Those in heaven gave 100 percent to everything they did.

Jesus asked him, "How did you like the service?" Roberts replied that he loved it.[8]

Tears of Intercession

As they walked along, Jesus began to weep. Roberts was astounded.

He began to tell Roberts holy, wonderful truth, some of which is too sacred to repeat. But Jesus told him that he could reveal one thing. Jesus said:

> "Roberts, I love my people so much that I would go back to earth, preach my three years over again, and die for just one person. If I had not already paid the price for them, and if I thought they wanted to come to heaven, I would do it all over again.

I would not have to know they would make it. If I just thought they wanted to come, I would do it for them, even if they were the greatest sinner of all."

He said repeatedly, "I love my people so much. Why do people not take me at My word? Do they not know that I have all power in heaven and on earth to back up what I said? It is so easy. I made it so simple. If people would just take me at My word, I will do what I said."

Then He cried harder and said, "I do not understand why people say they believe I will do something, but when it does not happen in their time, they begin to doubt My word. If they will just believe and say with confidence that I will do it, I will do it at the correct time."[9]

Roberts always remembers the tears of intercession that Jesus shed.

They continued on and arrived at a branch of the river of life. They walked into it, knee-deep and clear.

The water flowed through them, and Roberts felt a surge of energy flow from the water and into his being.

Then, Jesus did something personal. He reached over and dunked Roberts under the water of the river.

So, Roberts got back up, splashed Jesus, and they had a fun water fight, splashing each other and laughing.

Roberts is honored that Jesus would take time to play with him at his eight-year-old level. That day, Roberts believes that Jesus became his friend.

When they got out, a great wind instantly dried them off completely.

Their next sight was another massive building. This building was "strange" in appearance and had lightning flashing into it and thunder from within.

Whereas they had talked audibly, this time Roberts thought and wondered what the building was, and Jesus' answer came immediately: "It is the throne room of God."[10]

In front of the building, there were flowers and trees. There were seven rows of flowers. The colors of the flowers changed constantly to all the colors of the rainbow.

There were also 12 trees, such as the tree of wisdom, the tree of love, and so forth.

There were two warrior angels in front of the door. They each held a sword with blades of fire.

A little farther, Roberts saw three storage houses, about a third of a mile from the throne room. They were long and wide. When they walked into the first one, Roberts was in shock. On one side, he saw parts of the human body, in the various colors of different ethnic groups. On the other side, he saw eyes of all colors.

The building contained all the parts of the human body people on earth need. However, believers have not realized the blessings are waiting for them.

Jesus explained that these were unclaimed blessings." He said the building should be empty, not full.

Roberts explains that people simply need to get what they need "by the hand of faith."[11]

Sometimes, we have to persist in prayer, like Daniel did for 21 days, persisting until the angel could get through to him (Daniel 10:12).

They walked on for awhile and were quiet.

Jesus faced Roberts and took both of his hands in His and placed His other hand on Roberts' head. Jesus then ordained Roberts for his work.

"I am calling you to a great work . . . I am ordaining you to a great work . . . Hard times will come, but take them as stepping stones, not as stumbling blocks. Go with power and faith. I will be beside you wherever you go . . ."[12]

At one point, Jesus showed Roberts' his past life on a screen—and his future life on the screen. Then the screen disappeared. Roberts knew it was time to go.

Roberts was turning to leave through the nearest gate when he heard Jesus say, "Roberts!" And he turned back quickly. Jesus stood there, with tears running down His face and His hands outstretched to him and said, "I love you!"[13] Roberts then left heaven.

On his way back, he meet his angel, who flew to him and introduced himself. He said:

> "I am the one who is with you. I'm the one who stands with you. I'm the one who assists you. I'm the one who protects you," listing the various services he performs for Roberts. "I will be with you, even throughout eternity, and I will stand by your side. There will be other angels who come and go throughout your life, according to the season and the anointings that you carry. There will be different angels, for angels and anointings work together."[14]

Then Roberts was back in his room.

THIRTEEN

Richard Sigmund

RICHARD SIGMUND is a minister, evangelist, and founder of Cleft of the Rock Ministries, based in Maxwell, Iowa, USA, near Des Moines, in the American Midwest.

Sigmund is a longtime preacher and has ministered around the world. He has appeared often on television and radio and has ministered with well-known preachers, including Oral Roberts, Kathryn Kuhlman, A.A. Allen, William Branham, and Jack Coe.

Richard began preaching as a young boy and worked for 10 years, from age 10 to 19, with the world-renowned Allen. At the young age of seven years old, Jesus appeared to Sigmund. Richard saw Jesus walk down a golden staircase.

When Sigmund was four years old, he was caught away to heaven while he was in his grandfather's house. Richard's great-grandfather was a Jewish circuit-riding preacher during the Civil War.

About his experience in heaven, Sigmund writes: "I can't explain it. I can only tell you what I saw. And language fails. It really is indescribable . . ."[1]

During his visit, Jesus told Richard this: "Don't ever forget how much I love you and what I have done for you. Never forget how much I love those whom you are going back to and the place I have prepared for them and how much I love them."[2]

In 1974, at the age of 33, Sigmund was in a serious car accident in Bartlesville, Oklahoma. Suddenly, he was in a veil like a thick cloud, pulsating with sound going through it. A force drew him through a glory cloud, where he heard singing and laughter.

In a receiving area, he saw a veil with certain people coming through it from the earthly side to heaven. He saw a man come through the veil and meet two women in a joyous reunion. He saw about 50 people waiting to receive a man, who came through the veil and quickly changed from an old man to a young man.

Richard saw a woman reunited with her baby she lost at childbirth. He also saw angels welcoming people to heaven.

He writes: "The love of God is so great that no person could know it all. It truly is beyond finding out, and only eternity will tell it all."[3]

Sigmund saw that the veil extended as far to the left and right as her could; he had the impression it was hundreds of miles long. Every few feet, there was a path leading into heaven.

He heard a voice: "You have an appointment with God," apparently spoken by Jesus.[4]

Richard was standing on a golden pathway. Two angels walked with him, one on the left (his guardian angel) and one on the right, who talked to him. The pathway was about six feet wide, in a garden that stretched as far as he could see, with rich turf-green grass that moved with life and energy. There were groups of people.

There were banks of flowers of every imaginable size and color. Some were the size of dinner tables, others were like roses and four feet across. Their aroma filled the air. He picked one, smelled it, and then when he placed it back, it replanted and grew again.

The sky was rosette-pinkish in color and crystal clear blue. He saw clouds, which actually turned out to be thousands of angels and people walking in groups and singing in the sky.

There was a park with many benches made of a type of solid gold, similar to iron lawn furniture. There were massive, striking trees at least 2,000 feet tall, of many different varieties. Some of the trees were shaped like diamonds. A Diadem tree caught his attention. It had leaves shaped like a teardrop, like a crystal chandelier. There was a continual sound of chimes from the leaves as they brushed against each other in the gentle breeze. He touched the leaves, and they glowed. The tree glowed with light and sound, both of them beautiful. It was aflame with glory. There were tens of thousands of people under the tree worshipping God.

Sigmund went up to a tree and was told to take and eat the pear-shaped, copper-colored fruit. When he picked it, another fruit instantly grew in its place.[5]

When he touched the fruit to his lips, it evaporated and melted into the most delicious thing he had ever tasted. It was similar to honey, peach juice, and pear juice. The juice seemed to cover his entire face but was instantly gone. Some trees had leaves shaped like hearts. He smelled the leaves which gave him strength.

The angel said, "Behold the wall"[6], which was very tall. Suddenly, they were at the wall. Like others who have visited heaven, Sigmund feels that travel in heaven is at the speed of thought.

The angel told him to look at the books. A massive book was sitting on golden pillars. The book seemed to be a mile high and three quarters of a mile wide. Angels turned the pages. Another book, on the right, was the Lamb's Book of Life. As pages were turned, Richard saw this, written in three-inch gold letters outlined in crimson, the sacrificed blood of Christ:

RICHARD OF THE FAMILY OF SIGMUND: SERVANT OF GOD

Next to his name, the dates of his birth and conversion were written.

The wall was filled with all types of precious jewels, diamonds, and emeralds. When he touched the wall, it caressed his fingers.

The gates were massive, seemingly 25 miles high. There were three tongues of fire on each gate, representing the Trinity.

Along the pathway, there were many beautiful mansions with numerous verandas on the second, third, and even fourth floors. Amazingly, people would float from upper floors to the ground, or they would stay in the air.

Out on a crystal clear and beautiful lake, people were out on the water or even floating below the surface. The lake seemed to be bottomless and giving off a glow. The water was alive. It had a texture and caressed Richard's hand when he touched it.

He saw millions of people in the water walking, floating, and swimming. They could breath under water. When they came out of the water, they were instantly dry.

Later, he learned there are four rivers. This lake is fed by one of the rivers, which is hundreds of yards wide and deep and shallow.

The pathway led to a street made of a clear substance, like a jewel intermingled with strands of gold. It was like a main street.

At times, as Richard traveled, he would get a glimpse of Jesus a little ahead of him. Jesus was talking with people, loving them, hugging them. People were adoring and worshipping Him.

In heaven, everyone has a turn to see Jesus. To Sigmund, it seemed that Jesus moved at the speed of light, almost being everywhere at once.[7]

Children in Heaven

Richard would see Jesus hug and talk to the little children. An eight-year-old girl, who Sigmund remembered had died on earth from cancer, spoke to Richard and seemed to be a kind of ambassador in heaven, going from group to group and singing glorious songs. She sang a beautiful song in a powerful soprano voice and choirs joined in.

In another place, in a courtyard by some homes, a young boy played what looked like a massive grand piano with a harp in the middle of it. People joined in and sang, and angels stood at attention, some of them raising their arms and worshipping. Sigmund was told he was playing for Richard, to show that children can learn things in heaven that are impossible to learn on earth.

Richard was told that talents and abilities God ordained for children were magnified millions of times over in heaven.

Another boy about five years old sat an easel, painting a picture of a countryside. The boy would literally tell the paintbrush what to do.

The newborn babies in heaven had the power of speech and could communicate fully.

There was a nursery with thousands, even millions, of newborn babies. Angels and relatives were tending to them. Amazingly, they grew up at a tremendous rate. All the children were very happy. Some wore little playsuits, and some wore robes. They walked and ran and played.

One game they played involved forming a circle, either small or large. A specific child would float to the middle of the circle, and another child would give the floater a little shove. All of them would laugh and carry on. Another game involved seeing how far they could jump. They would jump 100 or 200 feet in the air and float down.

They would climb trees and jump out of them, floating down like cotton balls. They would play along the shores of the seas and lakes. They would play in, on, and under the water. They would swim through the water or sit on the bottom of the lake. They would play with the rocks and build sand castles.

They would also have footraces, running at very fast speeds. They would ride horses, which loved it and loved the children. The horses had the power of thought and speech. The children also played hide-and-seek.

As the children get older they attend school. They are far above the highest level of intelligence on earth and learn things that geniuses could not possibly understand. Sigmund was speechless. He was not allowed to know how fast children grow up.

Richard saw a group of children telling a glory cloud what to become. Jesus was there and told them something to do and blew on the cloud. The cloud became "an explosion of glory" and two beautiful, pure white, parrot-like birds flew out of it. The birds were about six feet high and immediately began to sing praise. This miracle was only one of countless events Sigmund witnessed which he is not able to explain. He was not allowed to talk to children except the eight-year-old girl.[8]

Heavenly Dwellings

Richard continued on a journey to the Throne of God. He took an avenue that branched off and looked to be 250 feet wide and miles and miles long. People were walking all over the golden and crystal streets, which seemed to be made of diamonds, with layers of gold and silver and precious stones everywhere.

He saw mansions beyond compare, which were for

missionaries. Richard saw missionaries arriving through the veil. Their rewards were great. He visited a mansion that was carved out of one giant pearl. The house seemed to be 250-300 feet wide and 100 feet tall. The furniture had been formed by angels who carved and molded the entire home. Even the chandelier, which glowed, had been carved out of pearl. The house was for a missionary named Pearl who was known for giving to the poor.

Richard passed by another mansion made of gold and wood. There were hundreds of people in the home—people the missionary had led to the Lord. The peace in the home was unbelievable. They knew Richard's name and greeted him, yet he did not know them.

There were many buildings on the street: mansions, smaller homes, and condominium and apartment buildings. No buildings had locks.

The acrchitecture was beautiful. The homes were brightly lit inside. Every home had large porches with pillars and massive archways. Some homes were made out of a type of brick or stone material, while others were made out of a type of wood. Everything was crafted and fit together without nails or pegs. It seemed that the houses had formed themselves into existence.

On one home, there was a veranda made of onyx, clear as glass. The porch was inlaid with precious stones, gold, silver, and diamonds.

Sigmund saw several large cities in heaven. Each city had wide streets, and one city had seven massive streets leading to the Throne. One house in that city was of clear stone with fragrant roses embedded in the stone, similar to the room in Rebecca Springer's heavenly home.

When Richard put his ear up to anything solid in heaven, he heard it humming beautiful songs. Some of the songs were ones sung on the earth.

The most beautiful part of heaven was Jesus. Everything dimmed at the sight of Him. When Richard looked upon His face, he forget everything else.

In the distance, Richard could hear beautiful chimes across the crystal sea. He very much wanted to go find out what was there but a stern look answered that desire. He was not allowed to go.

Richard did see a crystal city made entirely of glowing lights of different types. The lights gave off rays of glory brighter than the sun. The whole city was filled with tall buildings, some of which floated in the air. Some were round, and one was shaped like a diamond. There were chimes and a bell system. There were choirs and angels singing from the heights. Richard still remembers weeping with adoration and joy at seeing and hearing these "inexpressible things" (2 Corinthians 12:4).

According to Sigmund, he cannot express in words what he felt and now feels.

Richard was taken to another home, not as big as others but still very large. He walked to the house and saw his grandfather and grandmother. They hugged and spoke. His grandfather said that Richard's house was close by.

Richard then saw people he knew on earth, such as the evangelists Jack Coe Sr. and William Branham. He saw other great preachers who were among the people, encouraging them and telling of the great things of God.[9]

Everything in heaven is centered around the Throne of God. Everything flows into and out of the Throne. All traffic moves toward the Throne. People deeply desire to get to the Throne and to talk to Jesus. Richard saw Jesus numerous times, but he knew he had to wait his turn to speak to the Lord.

Walking down a street, Richard saw a wonder in a picture window of a beautiful home: a magnificent tapestry that a woman was weaving. In the house, the tapestry was hanging in midair without any support. The woman had a massive yarn-like material that she was speaking softly to, telling it what to do. She was creating a tapestry of what she saw from her window.

The image on the tapestry had depth, as if you could walk into it. The image was of the scene out the window, including people walking, people in groups singing, the trees and more. The woman had made it on the day that Sigmund was born again. Richard wept when he heard this. The angel smiled, and Richard realized that angels' highest joy is to serve God and be on assignment for the Lord. They weep with joy when a person receives Christ as Savior. Hebrews 14:1 says "Are angels not all ministering spirits sent forth to minister for those who will inherit salvation?"

Richard was taken to a testimony service with thousands in attendance. His grandfather gave a testimony about Richard himself, who wept and had a reunion with family members.

Instantly, he was in another place and was told, "You have an appointment with destiny."

Richard saw a group of 14 warrior angels, 20 feet tall and ten feet across at the shoulders. Their eyes were fiery. Their swords were flames of fire. The ground shook when they passed by. The angels with Richard stepped aside and bowed their heads in respect.

Jesus spoke in His strong, firm, yet gentle voice, "I wanted you to see them. They are being sent into your future. They will be there when you need them." Richard wept, and the angels referenced Psalm 91:11-12.

Then, Jesus was surrounded by children. He said, "Look at this," and He threw a large glory cloud into the air, which rose about 2,000 feet and exploded into what looked similar to fireworks, which got bigger and bigger and took on the shape of a tree, slowly floated to the ground, rooted into the ground and began to grow. All the people watched in awe.

Jesus said to the angels, "Take Richard to My marriage supper feast," and Richard instantly went there.

More Heavenly Buildings

He was at a very tall building with arched supports and columns. There was a pavilion about 20 miles long. The table for the feast was made of gold and inlaid with jewels. The chairs looked like kings' thrones and were engraved with names. The Lord explained the names were added when they were recorded in the Lamb's Book of Life. Richard's name was engraved, and he wanted to sit there but was not allowed. Goblets were filled with sweet nectar. Everything was perfection. There was room for millions of people.[10]

Richard was taken to a very large building, inside of which were rows and rows of shelves that seemed to be miles and miles high. The books were 15 feet tall. Hundreds of angels were servicing the books. The building was the Archives of Heaven (Revelation 20:12).

The books record our actions. Richard believes that when we repent, our previous sins are erased.

Another very large building with books corresponding to every person on earth. According to Richard, every thought and action of a person is recorded in heaven. There were many books for each person. Angels eight to nine feet tall wrote in the books using a five foot long golden quill.

Angels pulled out books which had something like a 3D video screen, containing histories of life.

The Lord Jesus explained to Richard that God orders our tomorrows, as we pray today. God gives us our tomorrows by a system of weights and measures. That is, we can know what is coming tomorrow because of checks and balances in our spirits. God has a blessing for us in the future. If we pray earnestly, it releases God to order our future.

Richard was told that all of our tomorrows are God's yesterdays.

Praying releases God to go into our tomorrows, lay a trap for the devil, and bring our blessings right on time.[11]

The angels told Richard that before the beginning of time, God created some of the things Richard was seeing. Before time, He created heaven and the host of heaven.

At the same time, while in heaven, Richard saw angels and people at work, creating homes and putting blessings that couldn't be received on earth.

Another building contained the written part of God's knowledge. He created this so that we could have something to relate to. There were individual symbols, with interpretations of the symbols.

A man in the room told Richard that he had been there for two millennia and had only gotten to page two.

Millions of angels as well as many other inhabitants of heaven go to the library. The angels go to this place to get wisdom. We can also receive the wisdom through the Holy Spirit.

There are many great universities in heaven. Our education on earth is just the beginning. Richard saw two giant buildings that were colleges. Angels and people taught others all subjects, including singing. The buildings appeared to be one or two miles long and one or two miles deep. The buildings could hold hundreds of thousands of people. The classrooms were actually massive auditoriums. He was told that everything you learn in heaven, you never forget. Richard remembers hearing many secrets of God being taught.[12]

Sigmund saw memorials everywhere depicting great victories for God. There were memorials to certain people, such as himself and to Cornelius, the centurion written about in Acts 10 who was generous to the poor and needy, as well as to Billy Graham and Smith Wigglesworth. They told of great battles fought and won for the glory of God's Spirit.

Richard saw Wigglesworth, and they waved to each other. Smith was helping people, directing them and telling them about the great things God had in store for them (Matthew 23:11).

Sigmund noticed that angels and people were serving others. He writes: "The way to 'go up' with God is to 'go down' and get beyond yourself to where there is nothing of you left. The death of self is worth much in the sight of God."[13]

The angels told Richard that God highly values someone who is honest; who prays before making decisions; who prays and seeks God in all things; and who is obedient.

Richard was taken to an avenue named The Way of the Rose. He somehow knew there were important events connected with this street. Some homes were under construction. He noticed a families' name carved above the entrance to a home. The homes were joined by beautiful lawns with flowering trees that must be thousands of feet tall.

The houses were three stories tall and contained exquisite furniture. There was a large lake behind the homes. There were also ornamental, hand-carved scenes of heaven, complete with live figures that moved and talked. The figures were cut out of a wood-like substance. The laws of physics did not apply in heaven.

The main libraries had books that were heaven's "pre-copies of books that have been written and that will be written in the time to come."

Jesus told Richard information about Paul Hegstrom, who founded and directs Life Skills International, a ministry that offers hope and help to victims and abusers related to domestic violence.

Jesus told Richard that the Paul Hegstrom home in heaven had books written by the Holy Spirit at the beginning of time. These books were given to Paul to write on earth. Jesus told Richard to tell Paul "there is much to do and not to slacken the pace."[14]

Richard saw Johann Sebastian Bach playing an organ

as choirs of heaven joined in praise and worship. The organ had notes far beyond the normal earthly notes.

Music was everywhere. Villages would sing specific songs, yet they all seemed to be singing in concert. He saw choirs from a distance, sometimes made up of angels. There was a specific song just for him.

Richard would see two or three people together singing and also large groups of people, such as a large group in an amphitheater, singing songs similar to songs on earth. He remembers seeing a group of 50,000 or 60,000 singing nearer to the Throne.

According to Sigmund, when you leave heaven, you lose some of your ability to understand the things you have heard there.

He learned that there is heavenly language that everyone understands. People also speak languages spoken on earth.

He saw stores which had specific needs for people, such a store with clothes tailored specifically to his own taste. Another store had clothing made before the beginning of time.

Sigmund saw a gathering place similar to a community theater. Thousands of women were sitting at tables and park benches. There was a pile of clothing in the center among the women. They were putting pieces of cloth together and telling them what to be, making garments for people. Richard believed the garments were rewards for people (Matthew 6:3-4).

Dress varied. Some wore pants and pullover shirts that were pure white. He saw other colors also. Some wore suits like earthly suits, though much nicer, while others wore long, flowing robes.

Jesus worse a long, flowing robe, with gold at the end of His sleeves and around His collar.[15]

There were groups of people in what looked like a band shell made out of a glory cloud. The shell was solid but clear and seemed to light up from the inside with a great amount of glory and all different colors, like fire shooting through it, with amber and gold, with sparkles and an aroma, the fragrance of God.

There was a homecoming for a pastor. Sigmund noticed there were balconies and bleachers in heaven that look over the events on earth. People watch prayers be fulfilled, births, weddings and so forth. They are the cloud of witnesses in Hebrews 12:1.

Richard was shown beautiful chimes which were like big towers shaped like diamonds, about 15 feet wide in either direction. The many chimes were multicolored and had massive pipes which made a full, deep sound. They were hanging on a pole which was diamond and about 500 feet tall.

Angels would rub them, causing the chimes to chime for about 20 minutes. People would join in and sing. Whenever someone got saved, they would chime a beautiful song.

Chimes were near the balconies as well. The seven large towers there had chimes hanging from them.

The angels took Richard to a very large building with many rooms inside, many of them mammoth in size. The rooms had extraordinary furniture and massive chandeliers, each one several hundred feet across.

A man sat in a chair like a recliner, reading out loud from a book to others in the room. Richard believes that the content of the book was about what a man on earth was going to receive in heaven for his work on earth, where he was a blessing to others. Sigmund believes that the building was evidence that God wants to bless us more than we desire to be blessed and receive from Him.

The chandeliers had a continual glow from within, like the Diadem tree, with an energy and in different colors like bursts of fire. Richard believes it was the Shekinah glory of God.

In this massive room, people were reading to others

out of books.

Richard was told that those who do not seek rewards on earth receive the biggest rewards in heaven. In this room, people were planning other peoples' rewards from books that were spoken, written, and recorded by the Lord.

Sigmund saw other large buildings, which appeared to be like factories. They were beautiful, with spires, arched doorways, and columns. The biggest building in heaven is the Temple of God, or Throne Building.[17]

There are fountains everywhere in heaven. Some were the size of a city block. The figures and statues in them were "alive" and were able to move. The fountains depict different things.

At a fountain, the water turned hundreds of colors and flowed over a mountain with trees. Mist sparkled from the trees.

Jesus was coming Richard's way. The angels stood at attention and backed away, bowing low with looks of adoration on their faces. Richard fell on his face. Jesus touched him, and Richard stood up. Jesus said:

> "Son, look at Me. I love you. Even though you have been disobedient and haven't done what I told you to do, I still love you, and I desire for you to tell My people about this place called heaven. I desire for you to tell My people the glorious things that My Father has made for them, that they might want to come here. I have chosen you and ordained you for this one work above all others that I might speak to you on this day of these things."[18]

Jesus took Richard's hand and walked with him. Jesus told him to tell people He was coming soon and that He loves them.

He continued: "Go with the angels. They are going to take you to see more people and to see more things. I have an appointment, and I have to go. My Father wants me: I must go. I am always obedient to My Father."[19]

Then suddenly, Jesus was gone, vanished and out of sight. The angels came around Richard.

Sigmund saw a fountain the size of a mountain, about ten miles in circumference at the base.

There was a duplicate of the cross of Calvary. There were seven layers of scenes carved in stone, such as the redemption of man. The scenes were alive and playing the complete life of Christ over and over. Near here was a glory cloud of the peace of God. According to Sigmund, this area was the third most glorious place in heaven.

The first most glorious place is God's Throne.

The second, and equal to it, is the Lord Jesus.

There were what seemed like millions of people simply shining in the glory of the fountain of God's peace, which reached to all of heaven and all existence. Richard was making his way to the meeting place. Jesus told the angels to take Richard to the living ark. Sigmund was immediately in front of a raised platform with an exact duplicate of the original ark of the covenant. Above the ark, there was a living statue of Christ suspended above the ark, with the blood of Jesus dripping down. It is a living memorial to the love of God.

Richard describes a "meeting place" where people initially go in heaven to have their first encounter with the cleansing of heaven's glory. The place is like a big amphitheater, with rows of seats, all looking through a large window that allowed you to look out over all of heaven. The view was breathtaking. No one was allowed to speak in the place.[20]

The City of God

Walking on a pathway, Richard started to float. He went through what he thought were clouds but was actually people. He could see the entire city and the Throne of God. He saw mountains that looked like they were 50,000 feet tall, with snow that never melted. The mountains had terraced parks. There were also "conveyances," which were like boats in the sky, made of carved wood and metal, carrying people.

The angels took him to the ocean, the Sea of God's Glory, which was crystal clear. Millions of people seemed to be in the water and under the water. One man had built a castle of rocks on the bottom.

Sigmund saw conveyances on the oceans, the seas, and the four major rivers, just as there are in the air. There are also land conveyances. Some are very large. Angels guide some of them. They are a place for people to sit and enjoy each other's companionship.

Up in the air, Richard could see the City of God. It seemed to be heaven's capital city. It was built around the Throne of God. It had beautiful buildings and villages in the surrounding countryside. The villages were hundreds of miles from the city and had different styles and flowing fountains everywhere. Buildings were suspended in mid-air, thousands of feet above the ground. Richard heard songs sung in perfect harmony.

Sigmund noticed there were layers in heaven. There was a layer with an atmosphere, with thousands of feet of air. Then, he noticed another layer just like the one below it. He was taken up to an altitude he estimates to be 30,000 or 40,000 feet. As before, he emphasized that you could travel anywhere in short moments of time. There were always angels and people around, and they were continually conversing about Jesus.

A very large auditorium was an announcement center. The Lord Jesus was on the stage. The place seemed to be able to seat 10 million people and was open to the sky.

The beautiful stage was made of gold, silver, ivory, and

a material Richard did not recognize. The stage had a throne, which Jesus was sitting on. There were bleachers and beautiful, hand-carved seats that were incredibly comfortable. There was a fragrance, an aroma that was indescribable. It was the fragrance of God. There were other announcement theaters throughout heaven.

Jesus walked onto the stage to thunderous praise, worship, and adoration. The Lord looked at people lovingly. Richard writes that "you could feel the Shekinah glory love that came out of Him. It was awesome . . . words fail" [21]

The people slowly quieted down to a holy hush. Jesus' voice was deep bass, like rushing water. Richard was not allowed to remember what He said, though he does remember that the topic was eternity and it's meaning and what God has in store for us.[22]

Sigmund had many questions. For example, he saw other levels that he did not understand. When he floated up into the sky, he saw another level of heaven, with ground, buildings, sky and so forth. He could not see it from the first level.

To Richard, heaven seemed like a very large planet, millions of times the size of the Earth.

He knew in his spirit that there were other continents, islands, oceans, and seas. He was not allowed to know anything about the seas, but he knew they were there.
Richard feels that heaven is multilayered. Sigmund saw four of these layers. However, no matter where he was, he could see the Throne of God in the distance.
The Throne is the "very center of the universe, the center of all existence."[23]

Though Richard obviously was allowed great access to heaven, there was much he was not allowed to do. He could talk only to a few people. There were streets he was not allowed to walk on and buildings he was not allowed to enter. He was told there are some buildings that people will never be allowed into.

After seeing all the wonderful things in heaven, such as houses, buildings, natural landscape, and so much more, he wondered how these wonders were created. He learned that the Diadem trees, which were miles in diameter, were made before the creation of the earth.

He was amazed that he knew every language and could speak to anyone with perfect understanding.

During his visit, he repeatedly asked the angels certain questions, and they regularly told him, "It is not for you to know at this time."

Finally, after many questions about the mysteries, the angel who did most of the talking looked at Richard and sternly said, "The mysteries of God are none of your business."[24]

In heaven there are prophetic areas, depicting things to come. Sigmund saw revival and judgment, including the black tornado of judgment.

A prophetic area had landscape that was rustic and beautiful, with mountains, rivers, waterfalls, trees, rocks and more. There were Falls of God's Glory, with a stream of water falling into vapor on the earth.

Richard was shown prophecy about the end times revival on earth.

Sigmund was allowed to see Abraham's amphitheater, like a football arena, but hundreds of times larger. It was magnificent.

All of the patriarchs had an amphitheater. Richard saw the Amphitheater of David. Richard knew in his own spirit that it was the place David and his descendants went to see their promises coming to pass.

Richard saw a building in the shape of a cornucopia, a horn of plenty. It was a Prayer Center, with much activity, especially angels traveling at the speed of light in and out of the building. They carried golden censers with prayers.

Sigmund also saw large fields of grain; thousands and thousands of trees filled with fruit, with people picking the fruit; a bank where giving on earth is recorded; and an area with supernatural, horse-like creatures.

Richard also saw a place with thousands of chariots and horses to pull them. The horses were white and about ten to 15 times bigger than earthly horses. They were all muscle, with crimson-red hoofs. He also saw other supernatural animals, such as a beast with the body of a bull and the head of a horse. An angel was sitting on it.[25]

Sigmund learned that God gives various leadership responsibilities to angels and people, according to His purposes. Richard saw more than 70 classes of angels. They follow orders perfectly. 95

While walking in heaven, Richard noticed angels of every description, busy with the people, doing the business of heaven. The angels were beautiful. They would stop often and bow their heads, in silent praise and worship of God.

Richard once asked an angel how time is measured in heaven. The angel looked at him with a puzzled expression and said, "You mean time as you know it?" "Yes," Richard replied.

"Time is not measured in such trivial things as years," the angel answered, "but in ages where the glory of God rolls on forever."[26]

The classes of angels were almost like family members. Their looks and clothing were different. Some wore shirts with drawstrings, and some wore pants. Some had shoes. They had hair (not below their ears), and some had beards. They looked to be about 30 years old.

Richard saw a group of angels that turned out to be warfaring angels on their way to do battle. Some of them were 12 to 15 feet tall, while others were as wide as four or five large football players. Some had swords but not all of them. All of them were massive.

Record-Keeping Angels

Another group of angels were keeping records. They were tall and slender. One of them was watching everything Richard did and recording certain things in a very large, golden book (Hebrews 4:13).

Warfaring Angels

Sigmund also saw what he calls the Armies of God. In an instant, he was taken to an area outside of the city and while in the air and looking down, he saw hundreds of thousands of angels standing in formation, lined up ranks and units.

These angels were not friendly looking but fearsome and dressed in battle clothing. They were around 20 feet tall and incredibly big and muscular. Some had swords of fire 15 feet long. They had large shields and 30 foot long spears.

Some wore short-sleeved garments, while others had long-sleeved. Some had on a tunic and pants with drawstrings around the neck. Some were only clothed with light.

They had supernatural weapons that Sigmund is not able to explain. They all had specialized purposes.

The angels with Richard said, "Behold the warfaring angels of God. They are mighty to the pulling down of the strongholds of the evil one." (2 Corinthians 10:4). Their hands were aflame with the power of God, so that they may accomplish all that God wants them to do. The angels emphasized that these angels are ready at all times to battle the enemy.

Sigmund saw them come out of the ranks almost at the speed of light and disappear.

Wisdom-Giving Angels

In another place, there were multitudes of angels giving to us for wisdom. The Lord Jesus and the Holy Spirit were in charge and guiding and directing the angels. The angels would get wisdom from the Library of God's Knowledge and bring it to people on earth or cause it to happen on earth.

Protecting Angels
Sigmund saw that born again believers have a vast host and even a multitude of angels who are at the disposal of the Holy Spirit on our behalf.27

Richard's angel companion who spoke to him the most told him that he, the angel, brought Richard to observe a certain portion of heaven. The other angel bowed his head in deep respect and adoration and began to praise the Lord. Richard was silent.

In front of him was the largest castle imaginable, seemingly miles in all direction. It was crystal clear and suspended in the air many thousands of feet above ground, with mountains all around.

When he walked through the massive gates, he saw thousands of people, heavenly beings taking care of the business of the castle. There were great rooms of books, with thousands of angels working in the rooms. There were three Diadem trees in the courtyard. The angel said, "Remember this," and Richard and the two angels were gone.

Later, the Lord took Richard aside and shared the meaning of the castle. He said: "That is the place where the hopes and dreams of My people are kept and fulfilled."

The angel spoke to Richard: "Your time has come to go to the Throne."28

In holy awe, Richard and the two angels were at the Throne of God.

Everything in heaven flowed into and out of the Throne. Everything centered around the Throne.

It was massive, beyond Richard's ability to comprehend. It was the biggest building in heaven. It seemed to be hundreds of miles wide and more than 50 miles tall.

There were millions of people going into and coming out of the Throne. They were praising and worshipping God.

There were flaming, living statues. There were a multitude of steps leading up. The columns were massive.

The closer Richard got to the Throne, the more magnificent everything became.

The Throne somehow faced every direction. It seemed to be 25 miles tall. From anywhere in heaven, you can see the Throne.

Millions of people were prostrate on their faces toward the Throne.

On their way to the Throne, the angels and Richard were in awe and were prostrate on the ground.

The Throne was made of a crystal clear material, consisting of what appeared to be gold, silver, ivory, and precious gems and jewels, all of them sparkling. Great waves of glory swept through it, like liquid fire. The building gave off rays of glory.

The light would have been too brilliant for natural eyes, so something was done to Richard's eyes to withstand it.

There was a Being on the Throne: "He was covered with a cloud of glory that radiated from Him: an all-consuming, enfolding fire that was the glory of God Himself. He dwelt in a fire of glory."

The glory radiated from Him, sounding like millions upon millions of dynamos of surging current.

Whoosh.

Whoosh.

There were seven large pillars in the Throne Room. There were nine pillars of a substance near to God. The inner court was surrounded by pillars. There was an area that seemed to be 100,000 acres with inlaid jewels.

As he got closer to the Throne, Richard noticed an area with a railing. There were three levels of railings, which humans cannot cross. Angels stood at the railings. There were living stones on fire. The stones were from the altar of God. They were about two feet in diameter and gave off blue and amber Shekinah glory. Every coal had a name on it. Richard saw his name and fell on his face before God. 108-9

Beyond this magnificence, there was a raised area. There were beings on the Throne. Winged creatures flew around the Throne, saying, "Holy, holy, holy, Lord God Almighty." There were flames.

Four rivers flowed from the Throne, flowing out from the glory cloud as one river and becoming four distinct rivers. The streams looked about a half mile wide. One of the rivers was the flow of God's mercy and grace.

Waves of glory flowed out from the Throne.

Richard saw memorials to the glory of God for what is done.

In front of the Throne, there was a laver, or basin, filled with the blood of Jesus.

When people get to heaven, they sometimes do not get to see God right away. They have to be there for a period of time before they can withstand His presence.

The fruit and leaves there help people withstand the presence of God. Every person has a God-designed purpose.

Suddenly, Richard was in a parklike setting, traveling at the speed of thought, moving toward a gazebo of some type.[29]

Jesus stood on a platform in a gazebo. He was about 180-190 pounds and had a reddish-brown beard. He had scars and open wounds on his face and neck. His feet were also scarred. He was wearing a seamless robe of light and was covered and surrounded with a glory cloud of light.

Jesus said to Richard, "I have called you as a prophet to the nations. In many ways, you have succeeded. In many ways, the evil one hindered you and overcame you.

But fear not: I have overcome him . . ." The Lord went on to tell Richard many things, about both his life and his ministry as well as about the great revival ahead.30

Next, the Lord Jesus took Richard to hell.

Richard stood by Jesus' side, while the Master talked to people. Then Jesus put His arm around Richard and hugged him to Himself. Richard wept uncontrollably.

Instantly, he was at the Throne Room. Richard noticed the fragrance of God that permeated heaven. He fell prostrate. There were things he saw and heard that he cannot express in human words.

At the Throne Room, Sigmund noticed rooms in a high, arched cathedral. There was a private area there where Richard saw his name and the promise of a covenant.

Next, Richard saw homes by the crystal clear seashore. The homes were floating above the treetops. Sigmund walked on the water.

He then went to a Rose Garden, a place with roses of every type and description, some with thousands of colors. Sigmund saw people he knew there.

Jesus told Richard divine truth. He concluded with this: "Go tell My people what you have seen here. And tell them to get their temples clean and full of My Holy Spirit. Only with My help can they endure to the end."

Finally, Jesus told Richard this: "You are going back. The will of My Father is never grievous. Stand to your feet. You must go back. You will come back to heaven. You will have angelic visits."[31]

Richard Sigmund returned to earth.

FOURTEEN

Mary Baxter

MARY BAXTER IS an author, minister, intercessor, wife, and mother, based in Taylor, Michigan, a suburb of Detroit.

Baxter is a minister at the Full Gospel Church of God in Taylor and has written nine books.

In March 1976, Jesus Christ appeared to Baxter, beginning an unprecedented series of supernatural experiences.

First, Jesus appeared to her for 30 nights in a row, taking her to hell. Jesus showed Mary the different parts of hell, which is in the center of the earth, and spoke to more than 20 people who are doomed to an eternity there. Mary was in shock and became ill during the experience due to the horrific nature of the visits, which would usually occur between two and five o'clock in the morning.1

Next, Jesus took Mary to heaven for 10 nights and 10 visits.

During these times, there were many other visitations from the Lord.   On the 31st night after these extraordinary events began, in April 1976, the power of

Almighty God fell on Mary. It was two a.m.

Mary was startled to see a mighty angel standing beside her bed. Jesus Christ was standing behind the angel. Jesus smiled at her but did not say anything.

The mighty messenger of God said, "God has given me a special mission. I am sent here to take you to heaven and to show you parts of it. Come and see the glory of God!"[2]

At once, Mary was supernaturally transported from her home and found herself standing outside one of the gates of heaven with the angel.

Mary saw overwhelming beauty that was breathtaking.

The angel's clothing looked like a brilliant garment of light. He had wings that glistened with the colors of the rainbow. The angel said, "Behold, the glory of the God!"

The magnificent gate was made of a solid pearl.

Two very tall angels stood outside the gate. They both wore shining robes and had swords in their hands. Their hair was like gold, and their faces beamed with light.

One angel went inside the gate and then returned quickly with a small book with a gold cover and printing. Mary felt like it was a book about her life's history. Her name was on the cover.

The angels smiled. They said that Mary could enter inside the gate.

All of the sudden, music filled the whole atmosphere, penetrating her very being. Waves of powerful music surged across the land and penetrated everything and everyone.[3]

The landscape was indescribable. Beautiful, colorful flowers surrounded her, with petals that would open up and sing. The greenery and vegatation was unbelievable. The grass seemed to have diamonds in it. The very blooms of the flowers seemed to be alive to the music.

There were trees with all kinds of fruit.[4]

Mary saw residents of heaven, who were exuberant. They were dressed in robes. Happiness and joy shone from their faces.

In excitement, Mary's soul praised the majesty of God. The sorrows she experienced in hell were far away.

She saw families of every nationality together. All the people were happy, smiling, going places and doing things.

All the people in heaven seemed to be occupied and busy. They spent time praising and worshipping God. They sang songs.

Mary could see diamonds everywhere. Some were very large, as big as concrete blocks. The diamonds were glistening and exquisite.

She realized that some of the diamonds were for soulwinners on the earth (Daniel 12:3). Mary saw men making a diamond for someone's mansion. The angels explained to her about who and why the men made the diamond.

At another time, she saw a hispanic man pour a liquid into a rose, and music came out of the rose. Other people designed a stone with flowers in it that would sing.

Mary saw carriers that carried people. They were shaped like a white bullet.

She saw the Lord's chariots. It was as high as a skyscraper and had wheels of fire.

She saw a massive, beautiful angel coming down a path, carrying a gold-edged scroll. He laid the scroll on a pedestal table made of a silvery material unlike anything on earth. A saint picked up the scroll and began to read.

He read, "Jesus is the Master Builder. He determines who deserves the diamonds and where they go. This scroll I hold is a report from earth of a person who has led someone to Jesus, who fed the poor, who clothed the naked- who did great things for God."[5]

The angel repeated the theme: "Come and see the glory of your God."

The angel stopped and told Mary that God wanted the angel to show her the room of tears.

According to Psalm 56:8, the angels catch our tears and put them in bottles.

Mary saw the room of tears. The angel took her to a grand entranceway that had no door. The room itself was not large. However, there was a holiness and power radiating from it. The walls were lined with crystal shelves and glowed with light.

The shelves contained many bottles, which looked like clear glass. Some were in clusters of three. Each cluster had a plaque under it with a name on it. The room had many bottles.

There was a man there wearing a deep purple robe. There was a elegant table with a majestic splendor, just inside the door.

Books were on the table. These books looked like they were sewn with the most beautiful silk-like material. Some of the books had diamonds, pearls, and lace on them, and green and purple stones. Mary was overcome with wonder.

The man told Mary to enter and see. He would explain about the tears and the room, one of many. He was in charge of this particular room.

A large, majestic angel entered the room. He wore a white shining garment with gold-edged trim down the front. He had large wings and was about 12 feet tall.

The angel held a bowl filled with a liquid (Revelation 5:8). The man told Mary that the angel just brought a bowl of tears from the earth.

The angel handed him the bowl and a piece of paper with the name of the person whose tears were there.

The man read the note and then matched the tears with the bottle with the person's name on the plaque. He poured the tears in the bottle.

The man told Mary to tell the people on earth about this process. The man took the bottle to the table, picked up a book, opened it, and poured one drop of the tears on the first page of the book. Words immediately appeared in the book. The words were elegantly written. Each time a tear dropped onto a page, the entire page was filled up with writing.

He closed the book and said, "The most perfect prayers are those that are bathed in tears that come from the hearts and souls of men and women on earth."

The angel with rainbow wings said, "Come and see the glory of the God."

They were immediately transported to a large area with tens of thousands of people. The praises of God became thunderous.

The angelic messenger took Mary to the throne of God.

She saw a massive cloud and a mist. Then she saw an image of the Being in the cloud. She saw the glory of God and a rainbow over the throne. She heard the voice of God, like the voice of many waters, and like the voice of thunder (Revelation 14:2). She saw many horses with riders.

Then, she saw a book lying on the massive altar. Angels bowed before Him.

Standing in awe, Mary watched as what looked like a man's hand came out of the cloud and open up the book.

Smoke ascended from the book. The most fragrant perfume filled the area. The angel told her that the book contains the prayers of the saints and that God was sending His angels to earth to answer their prayers. Everyone was praising and magnifying God.

As God opened the book, pages came out and flew into the hands of the angels on horses. Mary could hear God's voice saying, "Go! Answer her prayers! Answer his prayers!"[6]

Baxter explains that there are three heavens: the skies with clouds, rain, birds and so forth; the second heaven, or space, with the sun, moon, and stars; and the third heaven, where God lives, the destination of the righteous (2 Corinthians 12:2).

Mary was overwhelmed in heaven. To her, the wonder, beauty, and glory of that land cannot be pictured by the mind's eye.

Blazes of glory shoot from everything. She could feel joy, happiness, and peace everywhere. She heard many voices singing praise and worshipping, including angels and saints.

The angel told her she had a mission to fulfill: she was to tell the people of earth about heaven. He explained that God was showing her just some of heaven. He repeated, "Come and see the glory of your God."[7]

The Throne of God

She sensed they were near the throne, and she began to see a panoramic view of events.

God's throne was high and lifted up.

The glory of God overshadowed the throne. The River of Life flowed from under the throne. There was lightning, thunder, and voices around the throne (Revelation 4:5).

She saw a rainbow arching above the throne (Revelation 4:3). The brilliant colors of the rainbow mixed with light to produce dazzling colors.

Radiant light and blazes of splendor flashed from the throne, reflecting into every part of paradise.

The angel told her there were many other things to show her.

Baxter was amazed to see a room of records where meticulous records were being kept.

The angel told her that God has angels keep records of every church service on earth and every service in a home where He is worshipped, lifted up, and praised.

God also keeps records of people out of His will. He records what people give and their attitude when they give.

The angel reminded Baxter to make a record of these things. He told Baxter that there were many things that were mysteries to me, as Mary was only seeing dimly (1 Corinthians 13:12).

They reached another part of heaven, which had a very long corridor with high walls made of what looked like platinum. Baxter was amazed at the brilliancy of light and glory that reflected from the walls. A word was etched on the top of the wall: "Storehouse."

The angel told Baxter the rooms in the Storehouse contained blessings that are stored up for God's people.[8]

The angel disappeared, and Jesus stood beside Mary. Jesus was taller than before. He wore a brilliant robe and sandals on His scarred feet. His face and hair were glorious and beautiful.

Mary asked Him about the rooms.

The Lord didn't speak to me, but He put out His hand and moved it toward the wall. At that moment, a large opening appeared in the wall. All around the edges of the opening I saw glory and power and light. Jesus said,

> "My child, these are for My people. They are for sinners on the earth, if they will only believe. I died to make them whole . . . Healings are waiting for people on earth. The day will come when there will be an avalanche of miracles and healings on the earth. Child, as far as you can see, these are supply buildings, or storehouses. The blessings contained here await the belief of those on earth. All they have to do is believe and receive–believe that I am the Lord Jesus Christ and

that I am able to do these things, and receive My gifts. When you go back to the earth, remember that it is not you who does the healing. It is not the vessel that heals; it is I. Just speak my Word and pray, and I will do the healing. Believe that I can do it."[9]

Mary's visit to the storehouses and Jesus' words are very similar to Roberts Liardon's storehouse visit and revelation during his visit to heaven in 1974.

Then Mary and the angel traveled at a very fast speed to another place.

The angel began to show Mary what happens in the spirit realm when someone is saved. They flew at a fast rate of speed to a small country church with about 30 people in the pews. Mary could see what was happening in the church service.

There was a mighty angel standing over the church as well as about 10 additional angels there. The guiding angel told her that a large angel is stationed at every church that is ordained by God. The large angel is in charge of all the other angels at that church.

The angels were stationed in the church. Two angels poured what looked like fire on the pastor's head. Several angels had scrolls and pens and recorded people's attitudes in giving, logging it in their books.

A man who was drunk entered the church and cried out to be set free. Men prayed for him, the man confessed his sins, and angels touched the drunk man's heart. The black bands of sin broke off him. He praised the Lord.

Mary and the angels traveled back to heaven very rapidly. They passed through the gate and went down a beautiful pathway that seemed to be made of gold and arrived in a lovely room.

They were in a long corridor that led to many other

rooms. The angel said, 'There are many of these rooms in heaven. These are called rooms of records. You will see what goes on in these rooms. We are going to the room that contains the name of the man who was just converted on earth.'

The angels quickly gave the report written on a scroll to the another angel. Several ladders were positioned along the walls of the rectangular room. Shelves filled with books covered the walls. It looked like a library on earth.

Angels, singing and praising God, stood in line front of a large desk, which was eight feet by four feet. A square cutout was in the center of the desk, which was overlaid with solid gold. The desk was carved with fruit and leaves. To Mary, it was the most beautiful desk one could imagine.

Angels were going up and down the ladders. They were continuously pulling books down from the shelves and returning them to their places. Some of the books in the wall were different shades of color.

Mary saw the two angels from the church standing in a line with the book of the man who was born again. The angel told Mary that the angels retrieved the record of the man saved and would go to the angel in charge. Every room has an angel in charge. All is done in order to the glory of God.

The overseeing angel wore a majestic headdress, had golden hair, and wore a luminescent white robe with gold. The angel had a wingspan of about twelve feet. He called over Mary and explained that she was allowed to see what happens when a person is born again—and that she was to tell the people on earth about it.

The high praises of God and bells ringing filled the air. The angels had books in their hands and were happy and laughing, waiting to talk to the angel in charge.

Mary's angel guide spoke had a message, with an entire record of the service and salvation written down.

She saw the name of the country, the state, the county, the city and church. The angel showed her the name of the pastor, how many people were in the church, the order of the service, the people who participated in the church service, and the details of the church offering. The paper had recorded the name of the man saved, the message of the Gospel that was preached, and the exact time to the very second he was born again.

An angel confirmed with the two messenger angels about the latter being witnesses to the man receiving Jesus Christ as Lord and Savior.

Mary heard astounding praise and shouts, as if all of heaven was magnifying God. She saw saints dressed in robes and arrayed in splendor, singing "Nothing but the blood of Jesus/Can wash my sins away . . ."

The saved man's book had page after page of the old writings washed away. Every page had been washed in the blood of Jesus. His sins were gone (Isaiah 43:25).

Two angels saluted each other, and the book was laid on a tray. Mary began traveling with the angel at a very fast pace through the corridors of heaven.[10]

Mary stood before the throne of God. Horns and trumpets sounded. A cloud of Shekinah glory filled the area around the throne. Thunder and lightning sounded and flashed. She heard "Glory to God! Hallelujah!"

The angel placed the book on the altar of God and bowed down low. The voice of God resonated loudly . . . "Another soul has been redeemed by My Son's blood. Another person has received eternal salvation through the blood of My Son."

The Lamb's Book of Life (Revelation 21:27) was on the altar of God. Mary "saw a hand come out of the cloud and open up the book . . . The man's name was written down in the Lamb's Book of Life."[11]

Mary was immediately taken out of heaven at the speed of light.

Mary saw the Lord take saints through the River of

Life, which flows from the throne of God (Rev. 22:1). Saints shouted "Glory to God" when they passed through it. Then she saw a countless company of saints being clothed in the whitest, most gorgeous robes imaginable.

Again before the throne, Mary could hear the sound of trumpets.

Twelve angels stood ministering before the throne, wearing indescribably beautiful garments. On their breastplates, jewels were embedded in their garments. On their heads, there was a kind of heavenly material with glorious colors. Trumpets announced the saints, one by one. There was an inestimable number of saints, angels, and heavenly beings.

Angels were praising His majesty continually. Mary heard a great voice saying the words recorded in Revelation Chapter 21:3: "Behold, the tabernacle [dwelling place] of God is with men, and He will dwell with them, and they shall be His people. God Himself will be with them and be their God."[12]

Mary saw a cloud of glory. She saw the hand of God come out of the cloud and begin to wipe the tears of the saints from their eyes. She heard God say, "There shall be no more death, nor sorrow, nor crying. There shall be no more pain, for the former things have passed away . . . Behold, I make all things new."[13]

Mary saw the Lord place magnificent golden crowns on the heads of all His sanctified ones.[14]

Mary Baxter believes God revealed heaven to her in order to give her balance. She had been to hell so much and had seen and experienced such horrible things there and in the aftermath, that He gave her the blessing of seeing heaven.

On one of her visits to heaven, Mary saw the storehouses of God. An angel spoke to her. He was very beautiful and tall, with rainbow-colored wings shaped like triangles. He told her that God had given him instructions.

They began to go up higher through the atmosphere and went through the entrance to heaven, again. Mary saw fruit trees loaded with beautiful fruit. When people ate the fruit, the fruit and juice did not get on their hands. She saw families dressed in beautiful robes, walking up and down the hillside, praising God.

The most beautiful music saturated the environment. Heaven was a symphony of music, with millions of perfectly pitched voices.

Instruments provided beautiful accompaniment: stringed, brass, and others. Many, many unbelievable anthems of praise billowed over the landscape and through the streets.

They went through an area with absolute green grass. There were massive clusters of splendid flowers, somewhat like roses. The flowers looked like they were singing.[15]

They passed a place with beautiful, white horses, looking as noble as marble chess pieces. They looked as if they were large statues chiseled out of boulders, but they were real and alive.

A woman was talking to the horses, directing them to bow their knees in praise to God. They did it. (Isaiah 45:23, Romans 14:11, Philippians 2:9-11, Rev. 5:13).

Jesus

Suddenly, Jesus was standing there. Glory and power billowed all around Him.

He seemed to be very tall in stature. His robe was unique and distinctive from the robes of others.

His piercing eyes were beautiful. He had what looked like a neatly-trimmed beard and very thick hair. Mary remembers looking at him and thinking that the tenderness in His eyes is beyond description. "The loveliness of the Blessed Savior was awe-inspiring and wonderful."[16]

Mary noticed that Jesus' eyes had taken on a troubled

look. She asked him about it. He said, "Look!"

Jesus waved His hand toward a building where Mary saw a large opening. From the opening, billows and billows of glory and power came flowing out. Mary asked what it was.

Jesus explained that the healings in the storehouses await the people of God.

Jesus spoke to her spirit: "Child, when you pray for somebody on the earth, pray for them in My name. Remember that you don't do the healing—I do. Ask Me to heal an eye or leg, and I will do it. Ask Me to straighten crooked limbs or heal sick bodies, and I will heal them."

Jesus emphasized that the blessings in the storehouses were for both His people and sinners.

Mary believes the blessings and healings are available to be claimed by God's people who ask in faith and in the name of Jesus.[17]

Heaven is busy and filled with activity and excitement. Angels are always engaged in useful, industrious enterprises. One of Mary's messages is to tell readers about the angels working in heaven.

From Mary's experience, the saints are also busy in heaven and always have work to do.

Another lasting impression Mary has is of the order in heaven. Everything was done thoroughly, properly, and with the highest degree of excellence. When she saw families walking on the holy hills of heaven, they were about the work of doing great deeds in the Lord's kingdom.

Heaven is perfect in every sense of the word. Perfect joy and peace fill the hearts, souls, and bodies of all who are there.

Everything in heaven has divine, perfect order and purpose. Both angels and saints are engaged in excellent, joyful service. They serve God day and night forever.

Saints in heaven receive a new heavenly body and

will never grow tired or become weak.

The angel showed Mary the carriers and chariots of God.

The carriers did the work of cars and vehicles, carrying people to various placed. The carriers were shaped like white bullets.

The chariots were studded with diamonds, rubies, and emeralds. They had very large wheels, almost difficult to describe, with at least two wheels on each side. The fronts were low and open like sleighs. The chariots seemed to be on fire, but they were not consumed.[18]

When God speaks, it seems that twelve very large angels stand in front of the throne. They all blow their trumpets. The angels are twelve to fifteen feet tall, and their garments are adorned with beautiful jewels. They seem to prepare the way for the Lord to speak.

Mary could see a thick cloud surrounding the mighty throne when the Lord spoke or proclaimed a message. Power would billow out from the front of the throne. To Mary, the voice of God was a mighty roar—but also pleasant. She could understand everything He said.

Mary was with the angel with mighty rainbow-colored wings. He wore a white, glistening garment, and his hair was like spun gold. Light and power were all over him. He told Mary he was to show her the place where children go and what happens to them when they die. They were high in the atmosphere.

Mary explains that there are some events and things she does not remember about heaven and/or were not explained to her. Also, she was only taken to certain parts of heaven.

The angel showed Mary a vision of a woman on earth having a miscarriage. Two angels appeared by the woman's bed with a beautiful basket made of white marble and pearl.

Suddenly, they entered heaven through a side of heaven and an entrance that Mary had not been in yet. Mary remembers being taken to a certain place in heaven, high up and approaching from the left side of the throne.

They were near the throne, and the angels set the basket with the child down on the throne and bowed.

Mary did not see God, but she saw a similarity of God just as Moses did. (Exodus 33:17-23). Then she saw a hand open up the basket. She was sure it was the hand of God.

She saw the hand reach out of the cloud and open the basket. The hand took the soul out of the basket and placed it on the altar. Then the hands worked on the little soul. When finished, a beautiful, perfect form of a human began to appear. When developed, the soul became a handsome young man.[19]

Mary believes that the only signs of sin in heaven will be the scars in Jesus' hands, feet, and side, a reminder forever that the Lord paid the price for our redemption. Mary saw what she perceived to be the top of God's head- it looked like wool (Rev. 1:14).

God breathed into the little baby, and it became a fully perfect creation. The angels began to shout and praise God.

Then the angel and Mary began to go high, high up the side of a place in heaven. There were beautiful trees with fruit everywhere around them. Flowers of every description and all kinds of birds were there.

They went up very high to another place. Mary saw a large angel wearing a long, white robe, standing beside a gate, behind a desk. He picked up a golden book from the desk and handed it to another angel. When the second angel opened the book, shafts of brilliant, sparkling light issued from it and began to flash like fireworks.

Mary then saw people shout, leap, and jump as they saw certain people. The angel explained that loved ones were recognizing their family members.

The angel then took Mary through a beautiful gate made with what looked whitish stone or marble.

An angel of the Lord said to Mary: "From the time of conception, a baby is an eternal soul. If a baby is aborted or miscarried or somehow dies, God knows about it. He has given His angels charge over them. We bring their little souls to heaven, and God completes them. It doesn't matter if a baby has been aborted or dies naturally. It is fashioned and formed into perfection by the mighty hand of God. If the parents of these children will live righteously in Christ Jesus, when they come to heaven, they will be reunited and will know their precious loved ones."[20]

Mary emphasized that the angels in heaven are large and mighty. They wear glistening, shimmering robes that radiate large amounts of light. They are powerful and sincere, with their minds set to obey God.

After Mary arrived in heaven, she and the angel moved very quickly. They passed many fruit trees growing by the River of Life. Every tree was loaded with beautiful fruit.

As they moved along, they somehow became part of the music which was heard at all times.

The angel told her that they were going before the throne of God to see the worship. Hundreds of people were coming. The hundreds turned into thousands, and the thousands into an innumerable host. Mary felt like her experience was like John's as described in Revelation 4:2-5, 10-11.

The most beautiful clouds, mixed with glory and beautiful colors, were billowing around the throne. There was a dazzling rainbow arched above the throne.

Mary was in awe. She saw an image of a man in the clouds. She knew this image was the representation of God. She knew man was made in His image (Genesis 1:27).[21]

Everywhere she looked, she saw people, praising

God. The River of Life flowed forth from the throne of God, flowing and like a sea of glass and sea of crystal. Mary saw horses—big, white, elegant, magnificent horses, without a single flaw. They looked like they were made out of marble.

The horses' backs had white blankets with gold edging and golden reigns in their mouths. There were ornaments on their feet and their tails.

The twelve angels standing before the throne had trumpets and musical horns by their sides. They had flowing, glowing garments, embedded with big rubies and many kinds of immense stones.

Then Mary saw many spectacular musical instruments, including harps.

A woman in the center of the group of horses stood still. The angels in front of the throne picked up the trumpet or horn near them and began to blow. Someone in heaven proclaimed:

It is now time to worship the King of Kings and the Lord of Lords for His glorious acts and His glorious power unto the people of the earth.

It is time to give Him high praise, to worship Him in the song and the dance, to worship Him with music, and to worship Him for His goodness.

He is God. He is King of Kings and Lord of Lords. He is the Redeemer of mankind.

The trumpets were sounding during this announcement. Immediately, the horses all bowed their knees (Rev. 5:13) and began to spin and prance before the Lord.

Mary explained that in worship, we shift our focus from ourselves to God. We realize that He is the One who can solve the problems we are facing. [22]

Mary knew in her heart she had a calling from God. The angel told that God allowed here to see these things so that she could record them and tell people the things which God has prepared for those who love Him (1

Corinthians 2:9).

Holy Creatures

She was taken up instantly into the heavenlies and through one of the gates, made of an exquisite pearl with designs in it. They passed the River of Life and people. Mary was taken to the throne. It was overshadowed with the cloud of glory and the brilliance of the power of God.
Mary heard the multiplied voices of many angels around the throne. The number of them was inestimable.
Then she saw the heavenly creatures and the elders (Revelation 5:11, 7:11); four heavenly creatures and 24 elders.

The Living Creatures

All of the heavenly creatures had large eyes, some in the front and some in the back. There were massive and unlike anything on earth. Each of them had six wings. One had the face of a lion; another had a face like a calf; a third had a face like a man; a fourth was like a flying eagle.

All of them were constantly crying out, "Holy, holy, holy, Lord God Almighty." (Revelation 4:6-11)23

When new souls arrive in heaven, Mary saw angels meeting them and leading them through the River of Life. The angels then escort them to a place where they are outfitted with gowns of salvation, which are robes of righteousness. Then, the guides lead them to the room of crowns, where souls are fitted with a crown.

She noticed beautiful tables and many books in heaven.

In the record rooms where angels record what happens on earth, Mary saw the angels literally blot out a soul's written record with a bloodstained cloth (Isaiah 43:25).

Angels sat in the the record room, with golden buckets and stacks of books in front of them. Messages from the earth seemed to be in the books as markers. Angels picked up books, and in their hands was also a bloodstained cloth which was mixed with glory, light, and power.

Starting at the first page, the angels expunged the written record of the soul. They erased the old history of the sinner and recorded that he or she had been born again.

Mary emphasized that she also saw the angels recording the deeds and actions of the saints, such as tithing and giving money.

Mary saw large chariots of fire driven by angels.

While ministering in a church, Mary saw angels among the congregation, nudging and touching people, encouraging them to give their hearts to the Lord.

Another time she saw a vision in which a preacher would speak the word of God which would become a two-edged sword as he spoke. His heart was full of the Word of God, the words would leap off the page into his heart, then become a sword as they left his mouth. People would be healed also.[24]

FIFTEEN

Roland Buck

ROLAND BUCK (1918-1979) was a longtime pastor in Boise, Idaho, USA. He was pastor of Central Assembly of God Christian Life Center from 1950 to 1979. Boise is the third largest city in the Pacific Northwest region of the USA. Buck was originally from Washington State.

After 29 years of ministry, Roland, 61 years old, began having supernatural encounters with God and angels. During a span of 18 months in 1978-79, angels visited him 27 times and gave him divine messages directly from God. During this time, Buck also visited heaven and the throne room of God.

Many angels visited his home and church and gave him messages to give to the world. Buck was in awe of the mighty angels. One of the frequent visitors was the archangel Gabriel. Another angel who visited was the archangel Michael.

Between June 18, 1978 and October 13, 1979, the angels visited about every two or three weeks. They would usually visit the Buck home in the middle of the night for two to three hours.

Within a year after his supernatural visits, Roland

Buck went home to heaven permanently.

Buck said and wrote that there was "such a holiness and ... awesomeness connected with each visit," that he is always reminded of the eternal God and His closeness to and interest in families.[1]

The angels are different sizes and have completely different appearances. Most were massive, seven or more feet in height, and likely close to 400 pounds. They appear about 25 years old but have been around since before the creation of the earth. Their voices are deep and rich.

Their skin and clothing are radiant, with a lustrous, shimmering glow, which is from the glory of God. Their eyes are like balls of fire, but with such warm compassion one can actually feel it. It seemed like they could look right through a person.

He wrote also that a feeling of awe surrounds him when he thinks about God's goodness in bringing these messages by angelic beings, who bring His glory with them.

In regards to what God looked like, Buck was mainly aware of the "brilliance of his radiant glory."[2]

A simple phrase that would summarize God's messages might be: "I CARE!"[3]

Buck emphasized that God loves people so much, He is much more interested in them than in procedure. God loves people!

The angels often spoke about the sacrifice of Jesus, telling Roland that all of heaven speaks about it often.

The angels taught Roland that the Bible's highest purpose is to reveal the character of God.

The angels shared beautiful, magnificent, wonderful truths from the word of God. When the angels visited, "a living panorama caused truth to literally come alive as it passed before" Buck.[4] They would back up their truth with Bible references.

Over and over again, the angels spoke to Buck about

the importance of families to God.

During an early visit, an angel told Buck that God always has a back-up plan for events which He has decreed have to happen. He will not fail. God will get His work done even if He has to call someone else to do it—or He will do it Himself.[5]

The angels explained that the enemy might plan attacks, but the angels go into action to clear the way, scatter the enemies, move away roadblocks, and let people know that God loves them.[6]

One of the angels was the same angel who is written about in several places in the Bible. The angel appeared to Zacharias with the message, "Your prayers are heard!" (Luke 1:13); was with the apostle Paul at his shipwreck (Acts 27:27-28:5); with Moses to scatter the enemies; and standing beside Joshua when Joshua asked, "Are you for us or for our enemies?" (Joshua 5:13) The angel responded with, "Neither one. I am the commander of the Lord's army." (Joshua 5:14)[7]

On another visit, Buck was halfway down the stairs when his knees buckled. Two of the largest men he had ever seen were standing before him. One of them told Buck that he was the angel Gabriel. A radiation of divine power came from them. Buck: "It is impossible to describe my feelings of awe and wonder. The second angel was Chrioni.

Gabriel told Buck beautiful truths, including: "We are constantly holding back the enemy and putting them to flight!"[8]

Buck looked out the window and saw about 100 big warring angels standing in the driveway. They were casually talking to each other.

Gabriel said: "Read the word, feed on it, let it become the Living Word to you, not just columns of truths and opinions of men."[9]

He discussed the different types of angels, such as praise angels, worship angels, ministering angels, and warring angels. Their highest function is to exalt the name of Jesus.

The angels spoke in a heavenly language and constantly picked up messages from the Spirit. Often, when hearing reports, they would laugh and become extremely happy. Buck assumed the reports were about great victories.[10]

The angel Chrioni even played with Buck's great dane dog Queenie, tickling her ears, getting her on her back, and having fun with her.

Suddenly, Gabriel said he had to leave and vanished into thin air.

Gabriel often wears a shimmering white tunic with a radiant gold belt, white trousers and polished, bronze-colored shoes. His hair is gold in color. Chrioni has hair like a man's hair.

During one visit, Chrioni said that God had given him permission to answer questions.

He said the angels are busy all the time. He said one of their responsibilities is to take care of the wicked and ungodly people. He said to Buck: "You can never comprehend the depth of God's love because it is too great!"

Chrioni was one of the angels who helped deliver the children of Israel out of Egypt. Another time, Chrioni and angels threw large ice balls on top of the Amorites, the enemies of Joshua and the Israelites (Joshua 10:11).[11]

Early one Monday morning, about two o'clock, Buck was awakened with the noises of angels in his home. When he arrived downstairs, he saw one of the most awesome sights he had ever seen. Four great warrior angels were standing in his living room, and there was tremendous spiritual activity going on.[12]

Gabriel was there to meet him and inform him of an attack that the angels were opposing and scattering.

Buck's attention was drawn to a special, massive, warlike angel who resembled Gabriel. His eyes were like pools of fire. Roland could hardly breathe and was in awe when he was introduced to the archangel Michael.

Michael had come directly from the presence of God. The power and force in the Buck home was so strong that it took most of that entire Monday for him to regain his strength. Buck: "The human body is not made to contain the force that radiates from an angel like Michael."

Michael and the three captains with him were receiving messages from the Holy Spirit and passing along messages in a heavenly language to angel leaders who were carrying out the battle.

Michael seemed more fierce than Gabriel. Michael had fine, chiseled features and light colored hair. He wore a white tunic with gold emroidery and a wide, gold belt. His arms, hands, and feet were a deep tan (Daniel described them like "burnished brass), and he wore a type of sandal.

It had snowed about six inches that evening. When the angels were leaving, Michael and another angel opened the sliding door to go outside. They took about three steps, leaving footprints in the snow, and suddenly disappeared.[13]

On one visit, while Gabriel and Chrioni were talking to Roland, a bluish shaft of pure light about 18 inches in diameter appeared from the ceiling to the floor of the study room they were in. Both angels fell prostrate on the ground for at least five minutes. Buck fell down in awe.

Another time, Gabriel gave Buck a round bread-like wafer about the size of his palm and about a half inch thick. Gabriel said it was a little gift from God for strength and energy. It tasted like honey.

Then Gabriel gave Roland a silver-like ladle filled with a water-like liquid. Buck drank it, and he quickly had an instant desire to praise and worship God.

During another visit, Gabriel explained that

everything God has promised is already completed as far as God's heavenly book is concerned. Gabriel drew a sketch of a picture frame with a small box in the middle to explain the truth. He said people should look to Jesus instead of their current problem or circumstance.

The Throne Room: An Overlay of Truth

On Saturday, January 21, 1977, at 10:30 p.m., Roland Buck was seated at his desk, preparing his heart for the next day's services. His head was down on his arm on the desk, when suddenly, he was taken out of the room.

A voice said: "Come with me into the Throne Room where the secrets of the universe are kept!"[14]

In an instant, he was there. The voice speaking was the voice of the Almighty God.

Buck had difficulty comprehending what was happening. He was nervous, and God told him to relax. He said, "You can't prove anything to me, because I already know you."[15]

God told him, "I want to give you an overlay of truth."[16] In a split second, they went from Genesis to Revelation, first looking at God's plan for His people. God discussed His character, stating that he will do nothing in conflict with his nature or his character.

He told Buck that His plan him is good, and it will be accomplished. He referred Roland to Jeremiah 29:11.

Buck writes: "God wanted me to see how he really felt about man; that he had man in mind before he made the earth; and he made the earth so man would have a place to live."[17]

God proceeded to give Buck a "glorious glimpse of the hidden secrets of the universe; of matter, energy, nature, and space, all bearing that same beautiful trademark."[18] It was a dazzling overlay of truth, giving Buck new, profound revelations.

He then told Roland he could ask questions. Buck's mind was whirling, as he was in complete awe at being in God's presence. Finally, he asked God if He actually made individual plans for each and every person.

In answering, God allowed Buck to see the vastness of His heavenly archives. Buck staggered at the billions of files. Then God pulled out Roland's file.

God "wrote down" 120 events which He said would happen in Buck's future. In reality, the list simply appeared, and Buck could remember all 120 events, as it was instantly impressed on his mind.

God allowed Buck to see the archives and record books for others, such as Cyrus (Isaiah 44:28-45:5), the apostle Paul, and Abraham and Sarah.[19]

Buck wondered if there was a book with the failure of Abraham or others. God responded, "I have no other book. I do not record failure in heaven." (See Hebrews 10:17-18)

The files were complete and meticulously recorded. Buck believes they are the files that will be opened at the believers' judgment.

Buck was taken to various peoples' homes on earth. He also saw angels in his church building.

In heaven, Buck noticed that everything was on a very light, happy, relaxed basis, with brightness. There was a complete absence of the piety that many people associate with a relationship with God.

God emphasized that we as people should quit worrying about God's responsibilities. He told Buck: "You worship me, walk with me, put your hand in mine, get your heart in tune with me and I will give you the privilege of moving with me. Let me take care of my business! What I have promised is my business, and I will take care of it..."[20]

God reminded Buck that the earth is a wonderful place, because the whole earth is filled with his glory.[21]

God told Buck about outer space, including empty space, the graveyard of stars, and black holes.

At the time, there was speculation about the empty

spaces in heaven. God explained that there is an appearance of empty space because the gravitational pull of stars inside of themselves is so strong that it bends their light rays back inside. Therefore, the stars go out and do not give off light anymore. The black holes mean that their light is out and cannot be seen. These black holes are the "graveyard of stars."[22]

God explained that when a person turns their thoughts inward, they become just like the stars, wandering in darkness. When a person lives for the Lord, their light shines. If they do not, their light ceases to shine, and they also do not reflect the light that comes their way.

The entire visit took only five minutes of earthly time. However, Buck writes that "there is something about the dimension of eternity that you can't quite identify with time."[23]

God showed Buck that there is an area between our final eternal abiding place in heaven and the earth from which a person can actually be brought back.

It was explained to Buck that God could return them to life if He Himself chooses—not that the person would have a "second chance."[24]

This is a place where a person may linger before they die. Buck referred to the people who have had near death experiences.

Buck actually saw a type of hallway, like a corridor or tunnel, between life and death. It was like a waiting room before going to a final resting place.

Roland remarked to God that this was totally against his theology. God replied that He wasn't trying to compare it to his theology!

According to Buck, God has a wonderful sense of humor, and there is a lot of laughter in heaven.

Suddenly, Buck was back in his office and saw

himself with his head on his desk. Until that instance, he thought that he and his body had been in the Throne Room, but in reality, his spirit man had been there.

He was shocked to find himself back in his chair, because he still had the paper with 120 events listed.

The paper was about as thick as a piece of leather and was white, slightly opaque. It resembled parchment and looked like it had been torn on all four sides. He did not know what
to do with it, so he placed it in his desk on top of other papers.

Buck went home and told his wife about his experience.

The next morning, he went back to his office and found that the paper had turned to ashes, almost like fur. Their texture was feathery, light, and fuzzy, like snowflakes, but not white. The slightest breath caused them to move in a lacy manner. He carefully placed them in an envelope, and many people were amazed at the ashes from heaven. A few weeks later, the envelope was empty.

God told Buck that the Bible's highest purpose was to reveal his character. He gave Buck two sets of verses regarding this: Jeremiah 9:23-24 and Exodus 34:6-7.25

During the angelic visits, the angels outlined God's Priorities:

First Priority: The Blood of Jesus
Second Priority: Fellowship & Communion with God
Third Priority: Jesus is Alive
Fourth Priority: The Promise of the Holy Spirit
Fifth Priority: Go Tell the World
Sixth Priority: Atonement of Jesus is Everlasting
Seventh Priority: The Return of Jesus

SIXTEEN

Gerald Landry

In 1979, Dr. Gerald Landry experienced heaven. Landry was a longtime medical doctor with a diverse career that took him from Canada to Nebraska to Texas.

Landry, about 50 at the time, was living in Tyler, Texas, USA, with his wife Denise and three children. Going about his day on a typical Saturday morning, Gerald felt a severe, crushing pain in the middle of his chest.

After praying, he and Denise were rushed to the ER where the medical staff began treating Gerald for a heart attack (MI, or myocardial infarction). The doctor told Landry he had indeed had a MI. As Denise placed her hand on his heart and prayed, Gerald felt the presence of God.[1]

At 4:13 p.m., Gerald was transported from the physical to the spiritual realm. He knew he was in another world, which is as real as this physical world. Landry believes his soul and spirit were in heaven, so he was able to see with the eyes of his spirit.

Furthermore, Landry explains that when you leave the flesh, your spiritual awareness becomes more acute, because the flesh holds down your spiritual awareness. As he explains, "at death your spirit is released."[2]

Landry offers some insight into how time on earth and in heaven are different. He calls it the "eternal now . . . Eternity is the present, the now that never ends."[3] On earth, we need time to help us function and exist. As history has unfolded, humans through physics and mathematics have developed specialized ways to break down time, even down to a nanosecond, one-billionth of a second.

In heaven, the past, present, and future are all merged into what Scripture calls eternity. To truly understand this dimension, we have to allow our spirit to join up with the Holy Spirit and go beyond head knowledge to heart experience.

During his visit, Gerald saw multitudes of saints, as far as he could see in every direction, all dressed in white robes. The people were transparent and were "floating" on what appeared to be a crystal mirror or cloud. Each person was holding a crown in his or her hand. They told him, "We were waiting for you."[4]

Jesus appeared to him. Gerald writes, "[Jesus] showed himself to me on the cross as if he were in the flesh, still with his nail-pierced hands and feet, the wound in his side."[5]

Landry feels that the sight of Jesus crucified signifies that in heaven, the cross will be remembered forever in heaven. Moreover, the salvation of the cross will last forever.

Gerald explains that his words are inadequate to describe. "If I tried to describe what he looked like, the color of his eyes and all, my words would be inadequate."[6]

Jesus looked at Gerald with a compassionate look full of love. At that moment, Landry understood the fullness of the love of God.

Gerald also saw the perfect obedience that Jesus has for the Father.

Landry writes: "Jesus spoke with a voice that relayed the same love his glance transmitted to me—such gentleness and tenderness. Once you hear it, you will never forget it."[7]

Jesus said, "Gerry, my peace be with you. You are healed. You will feel no pain. You will have no anxiety . . . Go and tell

... everyone you come in contact with; tell them about my love."[8]

Jesus told Gerald to read the Gospel of John, the first two letters of John, and all of Revelation. Landry asked him why he asked him to do this.

He said, "John is my friend. He knows all about my love."[9]

When Jesus finished talking to him, Landry was back in his body on earth. His heart had stopped for four minutes, and he was brought back to life. After returning, he was in a coma for ten hours. Though he died and endured very traumatic and severe health crises, Gerald was completely healed after his experience.

SEVENTEEN

Ian McCormack

IAN MCCORMACK IS pastor at Kingsgate Church in London, England, United Kingdom. He is originally from New Zealand.

In 1982, McCormack was an atheist and enjoyed adventure. An experienced deep sea diver, he joined a group one day to dive, though he felt uneasy about going. He did not know that he would actually die, visit heaven, and then return to the earth.

Ian's mother was a believer in Jesus Christ and had always prayed for her son, though at the time of this supernatural experience, he was rebellious and anti-God.

While diving that day, Ian was bitten by two deadly box jellyfish, also called a sea wasp or marine stinger. The sea wasp, known for it's box-like body and tentacles, is among the most venomous creatures in the world.[1]

The bites sent poison through his body. Ian made it to the shore and was rushed to the nearest hospital.

Before the trauma of the event, his mother was alerted to pray for her son. While he was struggling to survive, Ian called out to God and tried to remember the Lord's Prayer his mother had taught him.[2]

After dying, he first was surrounded by darkness and apparently visited hell. Then a brilliant light shone upon him and drew him up supernaturally. God later told him that his death-bed prayer saved him. He was drawn into a circular opening above him.

He looked down a tunnel and saw a light with an awesome radiance, power, and purity. Parts of this light came toward him and went through his being. Ian now saw that his hand was like a spirit form, full of this light. He was filled with pure joy and excitement.[3]

Continuing on, seeing ever-increasing indescribable brilliant light, a voice asked him if he wanted to return. Ian said yes. In response, the voice told him, "If you wish to return, you must see in a new light."[4] These words appeared before him: "God is Light, and in Him there is no darkness at all." (1 John 1:5).

Realizing the light was from God, Ian realized he did not deserve to be there. He knew he was a sinner. Nevertheless, wave after wave of pure light flooded him.
Every confession he made brought another wave, and he stood weeping as God's love washed through him. He had a strong desire to step into the light and see God.

As he walked closer and closer, the light opened, and he saw a Man with dazzling white garments. Light emanated from His entire face, "like brilliant jewels with light and power shooting out from every facet."[5] Ian was in total wonder at the brilliance and purity of Jesus.

Jesus moved a little, and Ian saw a what looked like a brand-new planet before him. It had the same light and radiance as God, as well as green grass, fields, a crystal clear river, trees, rolling hills, mountains, blue skies, and meadows with flowers and trees. To Ian, it looked like the Garden of Eden or paradise. Ian wanted to explore it and stepped forward to go, but Jesus stepped in front of him and asked, "Ian, now that you have seen, do you wish to step in, or return?"[6]

Ian thought and realized he wanted to tell his mother

she was right, that what she believes is real. He told God he wanted to go back to tell her that.

Later, Ian realized that in heaven, he had seen all his family and thousands of people stretching into the distance. God said that if Ian did not return to earth, many of those people would not hear about Him. Ian responded (surprisingly) that he, Ian, did not love them. God said, "But I do, and I want them to come to know Me."

Ian asked how he could get back to earth. God told him to tilt his head, feel liquid running from my eye, and then open it and see. Ian found himself on earth, with his right eye open, lying on a table in a hospital. He had been dead for 15 minutes, but now he was alive. For the next four hours, he felt warmth and power flowing through his body. He walked out of the hospital the next day, healed.

McCormack is an ordained minister and has shared his story around the world.

EIGHTEEN

Yong Gyu Park

Yong Gyu Park was a Korean pastor, writer, and church leader who visited heaven in 1987. Park was a longtime Presbyterian pastor of a church with more than 5,000 members. He was also a wealthy businessman and landowner.

One day, he began having excruciating pain related to his high blood pressure and ended up in the hospital. While there, he died. After coming back to life later, Park could not speak for four years. He lived for another 20 years after his death and visit to heaven.

On that day in the hospital, two angels entered his room and told him Jesus had commended them to come to earth and take Yong to visit heaven and hell. The cries of Park's family made a difference, and Jesus decided to give him more time on earth.

The angels, one whom was his guardian angel who had been with him from birth until now, grabbed his hands, and they flew through the skies and clouds to heaven. Up ahead, Park saw other souls flying to heaven. The angels sang, and Yong Gyu joined in.

The scene of heaven was indescribable and beyond human words. Yong thanked the Lord. God's voice was overflowing with love and tenderness.

The Lord asked Park five questions, related to his prayer, Bible reading, evangelizing, tithing and so forth.

Park was not allowed to see the Lord's appearance.

The angels took him to three places: the place where the children live; the place where the adults live; and the place where people who barely made it in to heaven.

The children appeared as kindergarden age. The children did not have their own homes.

Most souls had individual homes, but some did not. The angel explained that in heaven, just like on earth, materials are needed to build the homes. A person on earth must serve the Lord in faith to earn materials for their home in heaven.

Yong asked, What shall I do on earth to get materials for my heavenly home?

There are seven things one must do: accumulation of worship and praise; time spent reading the Bible; time spent praying; time spent evangelizing; one's offering to the Lord; obedient tithes to God; time spent serving the church in any way.

The garden of flowers was beautiful beyond description.

He then visited the place for faithful adults. There were many, many homes built with beautiful gems and stones. Some homes were as high as skyscrapers. Those who were faithful on earth had their homes built here.

Yong met a man who had suffered from a disease on earth. In heaven, he was completely healthy.

Park then rode a golden chariot to the place for those who were shamefully saved. The village was enormous, several times bigger than the second place, and far away.

There were massive, wide, flat houses that were like a big warehouse. The buildings were shabby. The angel said he wanted to show Park two houses: one was for pastors on earth, and one for elders on earth.

The angels emphasized the importance of service and sacrifice. They also said that if someone gets a reward and recognition on earth for any good deed, they will not get a reward in heaven.[1]

NINETEEN

Jesse Duplantis

JESSE DUPLANTIS IS founder of Jesse Duplantis Ministries, an evangelistic ministry based in New Orleans, Louisiana, USA.

In 1988, Duplantis was taken to heaven, where he experienced the glories of heaven, spent time with Jesus, met and spoke with several patriarchs of the faith, and much more.

Duplantis is a Cajun, an ethnic group in Louisiana, and is originally from the Bayou Country there, from the town of Houma, one hour from New Orleans. Houma is known for having more than 2,500 square miles of mysterious swampland and wetlands. Duplantis, known for his entertaining style and background in music, appears often on television.

Before his heavenly visit, Duplantis had experienced the supernatural, such as seeing as many as 100 angels in one of his services. One night, an angel visited his bedroom.

In August of 1988, Duplantis was preaching a revival meeting in Magnolia, Arkansas, USA. On one morning when he awoke, Duplantis felt an uneasy feeling, similar to a feeling of nervousness with extra adrenalin.

On that August day in Arkansas, Duplantis was at lunch when he felt compelled to return to his room. He left the lunch, went into his room, and noticed that it was 12:59 p.m.

Suddenly he felt a suction like he was being pulled out of the room. He heard a sound, *Whoosh!* And he was pulled up out of the hotel room. He gasped, "Aaah . . ."

Jesse was zooming through the skies at a phenomenal rate of speed in something similar to a cable car. He was completely closed in. He could see through the windows that the chariot-like car was moving very fast, but he did not know how it was being operated.

Looking up, he saw an angel—the same blond-haired angel who had visited him in his bedroom years before.

Jesse asked, "Where are we going?"

The angel smiled and said, "You have an appointment with the Lord God Jehovah."[2]

The chariot slowed down and stopped. The door opened. Jesse was in shock: he was in heaven.

The first thing Jesse saw was Paradise, a beautiful place that surrounds the Holy City. As Jesse fell to the ground praising God, the angel also fell down, praising the Most High God Jehovah.

Everything was beautiful. Surrounded by light, Jesse saw lush valleys, many mountains, flowers he had never seen, snow, and streams of water. He saw colors he had never seen before—reds, greens, purples, blues, yellows, gold as clear as crystal.

There were trees lined up next to the River of Life. Thousands of people stood under the trees. He saw children, horses, dogs, and cats like lions. Everyone was headed to God's Throne, which was high and lifted up and could be seen from every direction.[3]

While Jesse was wearing jeans and a shirt, many people were wearing glorious robes or gowns. When they got out of the chariot, they shouted and praised God as they ran to the throne.

Those with gowns seemed to get weak as they walked toward the throne. So they ate fruit and smelled leaves from the trees. The angel explained, "Some of them have not lived the life they should. They believe in God and love Jesus, but they didn't live to their fullest potential . . . They have to be prepared to stand in the presence of the Almighty."[4] (Revelation 22:1,2)

The angel explained that when they eat fruit, the people are strengthened. As they get closer to the city, the anointing and the light will get stronger. Before the throne, the light can be blinding.

A man stepped out of a chariot wearing a gown and cried out, "I didn't think I was going to make it, but I did!" He kissed the ground.[5]

When Jesse asked if the man would make it to the throne, the angel replied: "He barely made it in, but our great God is merciful!"[6]

The gowns were beautiful. Duplantis cites Isaiah 61:10,11 which refers to the garment of salvation and the robe of righteousness.

When Jesse would get weak, the angel would pick some fruit and give it to Duplantis. The fruit was juicy and copper-colored.

The angel offered Jesse something to drink. The angel dipped a gold goblet into the river, which was pure and clear and the size of a creek or a big stream.

Duplantis saw a large, big-chested, young-looking man. Jesse knew in his spirit it was Abraham.

Abraham walked over to Jesse and the angel, giving Jesse the goblet and saying, "Hey, Jesse! Drink this."[7]

Jesse fell down on his face before him, and Abraham said, "Stand to your feet The only One you worship is the Lord God. I'm a servant. I have come to help you. I meet all the people who come here because Paradise is my bosom."[8] Jesse drank the cool and refreshing water

Abraham gave him.

As they walked along, the flowers' beauty and fragrance were beyond human words. Amazingly, the flowers were not crushed when he walked on them. When they walked by, the flowers turned towards them so the passer-by could always see their beauty.

Noticing he did not have a shadow, Jesse wondered about it, and the angel replied, "In this place, there is no darkness. God is Light in Whom there is no darkness, no shadow of turning." (James 1:17)[9]

Looking everywhere, Jesse could not find a shadow. Jesse asked about the fragrance. The angel that in heaven, the fragrance of God is in everything.

Suddenly, he heard and saw children singing, praising, and carrying harps.

The angel said, "These are children that the earth did not want. God brought them here . . . children must be taught the oracles of God."[10] The children were about three to 10 years old.

The kids started saying, "He's coming!"[11] Suddenly, he saw a light coming from the city. He saw Jesus reaching out to the kids as they sang and hugged Him, adoring Him.

The angel told Jesse they must go to the city. The angel had fruit for Jesse and offered it frequently. Some people in gowns were trying to make it to the city but were weak and had to turn back. The people in robes were marching into the city.

As they approached the city, they came to the jasper wall described in Revelation 21. Jesse told the angel that he wanted to see the names of the apostles. On the pillars, he saw: Peter, Paul, James, and John. He wanted to stay there but the angel had him get into the chariot.

Just inside the city, Jesse saw the Book of Life. It was large, about five and a half feet tall and one or two inches thick. The binding was like a gold cloth.

The angel stopped the chariot and said "Kneel. He's

here."[12] Jesse felt weak and fell to his knees. As Jesus approached, the children ran up to him, praising and celebrating. Jesus rejoiced with them.

Jesus was like a shaft of light. He turned toward Jesse, who fell at His feet.

Kneeling down, he noticed that Jesus feet were like burnished brass. There were holes in his feet from the crucifixion.

A brilliance came out of Jesus that seemed like waves of glory. Light was shining from him. His clothing looked like solid, sparkling diamonds.

He was about 5'11" to 6'1", with white hair that also looked light brown when he turned. Jesse called out Jesus' name.

"Do you like this place?" Jesus asked him.

"Yes, sir."

Jesse confessed that he had made mistakes.

"You're forgiven. I made a plan of redemption."

Jesse asked why he was in heaven.

"I want you to go back and tell My people I'm coming."

"But they won't believe me."

"They didn't believe it for centuries, but I came, and I am coming again."

Jesus told him twice more to "go tell My people I'm coming."[13]

Duplantis describes Jesus as "beautiful . . . Glory is emanating from Him. His eyes are like pools of love, and He is the color of light."[14]

Sometimes, a thought would come to Jesse's mind, and Jesus would answer it before Jesse could speak.

David, Paul and Jonah

With His arm around Jesse, Jesus told him, "I want you to meet another king." Jesse knew right away it was David, who spoke to Jesus, "To the great King of kings I bow."[15]

Jesus introduced Jesse and asked David to take Jesse to Duplantis' home, then to the throne. Jesus told them, "I must go. My Father wants Me."[16]

Jesse bowed down, "Oh, king!"

"Don't bow to me. You just looked at the King of kings. I've been assigned to take you around."[17]

Jesse asked him how he could help David, who replied that everyone in heaven is a servant. He asked Jesse: "What do you want, Jesse? What do you need?"[18]

They walked into a house with a beautiful foyer. By the wall in a corner, they saw the apostle Paul sitting with several men. Paul was somewhat short in stature.

"Jesse!" said Paul. Jesse could not believe that Paul knew his name.

"Jesse, what are they saying about my gospel?"

Jesse was attracted to Paul's knowledge, complimenting him for his great intellectual mind. Paul was humble, "The Lord has been gracious to me."

After talking for a little bit, Paul said, "Our affliction is but for a moment. People have made it a lifetime. Change it back to a moment."

Paul continued, "Change it back to a moment, Jesse." Then he whispered, "Change it back to a moment. Don't leave it a lifetime. I've kept the faith, and that's how it's done. And it worked. " (2 Corinthians 4: 17,18)

He also added, "Never change the message because of the hearers. Speak what God gives you."[20]

Jesse and David had some good laughs. David was the only person other than Jesus with a crown on his head. People showed him great respect and even awe. David had a big smile and a hearty laugh.

Duplantis asked him how he got his ideas for his songs.

"From the Lord. I did write songs of my experiences, like a lot of other people do. But the better ones are when I allowed the lordship of God in me to come out more than the trouble that I spoke about."²¹

"I wish I had written more songs about God's answers than about my problems. If I had listened to the Lord, there are some things I would have never gone through. Now you have my record, so follow the record God told me and you won't walk through some of the places I walked through."²²

David took Jesse to the latter's house. The grounds were well-manicured and had a water fountain. In the foyer, there were tall ceilings and crown moldings. The house was decorated just like Jesse likes it. There was marble and a table with golden eagles.

Jesse was very appreciative of the house. When Jesse said he liked the furniture, David told him:

"Yes, the Lord knew you would like it, so we put it in your home. We told you He would give you the desires of your heart. All desires are met here. Everything has been thought of—all your desires and some that you could not even think of."²³

Jesse remarked that there are lots of things in heaven that look like things on earth.

"Well, the earth is the Lord's taste," said David. "Remember, he created it. So a lot of what you see there you will see here." ²⁴

They met a family who had died in a plane crash. They invited Jesse to go on a picnic, but he could not go because of his appointment.

David then took him down a street where the prophets live. They knew Duplantis' name, and Duplantis asked David how they knew him.

David explained that they know him because Jesse has preached their sermons and that God blesses them with knowing their messages are reaching people.

Duplantis then got to speak with the prophet Jonah and asked him about being in the whale.

"I was in disobedience," said Jonah. "Disobedience is a powerful thing against you. Not only in the life that you live now, but here."

"God's word must be followed to the letter."[25]

In the famous story, God had told Jonah to go to the city of Nineveh to preach against its sins in order to lead them to repentance and salvation. Jonah disobeyed and spent three days in a whale. After coming out of the whale, God re-issued his command to Jonah to preach to the Ninevites. This time Jonah obeyed. After hearing Jonah's preaching, the people of Nineveh did repent, and God had compassion and withheld judgment.

Jonah explained that after coming out of the whale, he was determined to obey God. When God spared the city, Jonah felt irritated about it.

Jonah 3:10 says, "Then God saw their works, that they turned from their evil way; and God relented from the disaster that he had said he would bring upon them, and he did not do it."[27]

Jonah continued in his conversation with Duplantis: "I felt irritated because I thought of myself more than I thought of the nature of God. His nature is not to destroy, but to heal and bless."[28]

The Throne Room

Jesse felt weaker and weaker as they approached the Throne room. There seemed to be millions of people there.

Near the throne, Jesse saw twenty-four empty seats (Revelation 4:4). David explained that people in heaven are servants, even the elders.

Several massive angels were flying around the room. They had chiseled faces and 30 foot wing spans.

As they got closer to the throne, Jesse became weaker. When the light from the throne hit him, he fell down. The angel gave him more fruit. Duplantis explains that God's glory washes out your glory as "His glory goes in and on you."[29]

Jesse could not look up for very long, but he did look

up. He saw his feet. The light was so intense, he had to look away and keep looking down. However, he did look again and saw the lower part of His hand resting on the arm of the throne.

"He is so big—you can't describe Him in a dimension."[30]

The form of God's body is somewhat like energy and spirit. The power, the energy-like smoke of God, covers all around the chair of the throne itself.

Jesse heard a sound like *Whooooosh!* There was a massive amount of energy, power, smoke, and noise there.[31]

The angels with wings were circling the Throne, singing and shouting, "The Great God Jehovah!" Every time they circled the Throne they praised God because they saw a new facet of Him they had never seen before.

Just as the seraphim in Isaiah 6:3 and the living creatures in Revelation 4:8 cry out, the angels express what they see by saying "Holy! Holy! Holy!" Even though angels have been flying around God's Throne since the beginning of their existence, they are still seeing new revelations of his glory, love, and character.

There was a cloud and a massive sound. Jesse saw God's finger barely move, causing an angel near him to be thrown against a wall. It did not hurt the angel, but he felt that if God barely moved, a universe could be destroyed.[32]

While lying on his face at the throne and getting weaker, Jesse saw Jesus Himself come out of Jehovah God and the massive power and energy surrounding Him. Millions of people at the throne fell down before Him.

At that moment, Jesse could understand the trinity. Then Jesus proceeded to preach with power, authority, and emotion. Jesus was torn with compassion for those on earth.

Jesus preached:

"I am going to get my body, and my body shall reside in this place my Father has created for us all. I'm going to get your brothers! I'm going to get your sisters! I'm going to get your family! I'm bringing them back to live with Me forever and ever!"[33]

The people were shouting and praising God.

Then Jesse heard Jehovah's voice, saying, "I am well-pleased."[34]

Jesse could not look at Jehovah's face, but he could look at Jesus. While preaching, at times Jesus would look back at the Father, as if they did not want to be separated. He could sense the love and affection between them.

Furthermore, Jesus would walk in and out of the massive energy there, and the form of a man would transform into Spirit.

Duplantis saw babies singing and even flying around God's throne. He realized they were new souls that God literally thought into existence.

The babies asked God, "Can I be a spirit? Would you send me to earth so I can be a spirit?"[35]

The mighty power of God—*whooosh!*—was there as the babies left the throne of God.

The angel said, "We must go. It's too strong for you. Come."[36] David walked with them.

As they passed a beautiful building, Jesse asked if he could go in. But the angel told him he could not, as no man had ever seen inside it.

Suddenly, while walking down the street of the prophets, Jesse heard a familiar voice call his name. Turning around, he saw Jesus.

Jesse told him that His message was great and wonderful.

Jesus replied, "It is a true message. That's why you

were sent here. You are to tell My people."

"They won't believe me."

Jesus was firm, "You just tell them. When they think it not, so shall I come."[37]

In reality, Jesse was disappointed to learn that his trip to heaven was for this particular lesson.

Duplantis even said it again, "Lord, they know that."

Jesus became stern and raised His voice, "No they don't! You go tell them I'm coming."[38]

There was intensity in his face and voice. Jesse realized that His coming is the greatest thing we can wait for.

Jesse confessed his failures to Jesus. "Lord . . . I've made some mistakes in my life."

"I don't know that you did," replied Jesus. "I washed them away. You're free."

"Thank you!"

Then tears welled up in Jesus' eyes. He said:

"The worst day of my life is yet to come....You know that scripture where I said I will wipe away all tears in heaven?"[39]

Jesus was referring to Revelation 21:4-5: "And God shall wipe away all tears from their eyes; there shall be no more death, nor sorrow, nor crying. There shall be no more pain, for the former things have passed away."[40] Jesus said:

> "Those include the tears in my eyes, Jesse. On that great Judgment Day, I will have to tell some of the creation I love to depart from me. I dread that day. I dread it! I dread it! Jesse, it's final. I can't change it. Tears flowed from my eyes the day my creation, Adam, fell. But I knew I would send myself. I had a chance to touch people. But that day is coming, and it's final. Once it's said, I can't change it. I have to wipe the tears from my

eyes. Tell them I'm coming, Jesse."[41]

Duplantis asked Jesus when he was coming back. Jesus replied that people should look for his witness and not the signs.

Jesus told him he had to return to earth. At that, the Lord directed David to take Jesse back via the mountains. Jesus smiled, and Jesse noted that his eyes looked like pools of love.

"I'll see you soon," He said. "One day we'll never part. It will be forever, and sooner than you think."[42]

On the way back, Jesse saw people having picnics, eating and enjoying themselves. He saw little apartments and condominiums. He asked David about them.

David replied that all desires are met in heaven. People have a home in the city as well as in the country. In the city, some people like to have an apartment as well, so the great God Jehovah has provided it. Every desire is met.

There were people of many different races. Jesse saw a group of Oriental children being taught by a lady. He asked David if their parents were there. David replied that some are, but most of the parents are not. People grow to an age when they have to accept or reject God.

As Jesse was leaving Paradise, Abraham bid him farewell.

Then He was on his way home again.

TWENTY

Don Piper

Don Piper is an ordained minister, pastor, author, speaker, and Christian leader based in Pasadena, Houston, Texas, USA, where he lives with his wife Eva. Before his roles in ministry, Piper was a television network executive.

In 1989, Piper caught a glimpse of heaven. Don was returning from a church conference in Texas when he was in a serious car accident, was pronounced dead, and experienced the heavenly realm.

Through prayer, intercession, many surgeries, and miracles, Don is now able to walk and continues to minister around the world. He has appeared on numerous televion and radio programs and featured in countless periodicals and newspapers. His book about his testimony has been a bestseller.

After the wreck on January 18, 1989, Piper's last recollection before his near death experience was a brilliant light enveloping him. The next moment, he was standing in heaven.

He felt a deep inner joy and noticed a large crowd of people standing in front of a brilliant, ornate gate. They were all people who had died during Don's lifetime.

All the people were smiling and praising God, and they rushed to Don. They were his heavenly welcoming committee.

Piper saw his grandfather Joe Kulbeth, who called out "Donnie!" and embraced his grandson.[1]

The crowd surrounded Don and hugged him, kissed his cheek, and shook his hand.

He also saw his friend Mike Wood, a dedicated Christian who was influential in Don becoming a Christian. Mike had tragically died in a car wreck at age 19.

Don saw many family members and friends. He saw his great-grandfather; his great-grandmother Hattie Mann, a Native American; his friend Barry Wilson who had drowned in an accident; two teachers who had talked to Don about Jesus Christ; and family members from his very large earthly extended family.

Warm, radiant light engulfed Don. He had never seen such beauty. According to Don, heaven's light and texture defy explanation. He could hardly grasp the vivid, dazzling colors. He had never seen, felt, or heard anything so real.

He was in another dimension. There was no sense of time passing.

Don had no awareness of what he left on earth and had no regrets. It was like God removed anything negative from his consciousness.

His great-grandmother Hattie was now fully healthy and beaming. On earth, at least when Don knew her, she had been slumped over, with wrinkled skin and false teeth. Now, she was radiant.

Everything around him glowed with a dazzling intensity. Human words cannot express the feelings of awe and wonder. Don noticed an even brighter, more brilliant light in the distance.

Everyone started to move toward the bright light, as they all walked up a gentle slope of a hill. Behind the gate, the light had a radiance and iridescence that made the light in front of the gate seem pale by comparison. He compared it to opening a door to bright sunlight from a dark room.

The farther they walked, the brighter the light got. He felt like he was being ushered into the presence of God. He was in awe.

Then he heard music, the most beautiful and pleasant sound he had ever heard.

It seemed like he was part of the music, like it played in and through his body. The sounds embraced him. It felt like a concert permeated every part of his being.

Don did not see what produced the sounds, though he felt like it was coming from above him. He had no questions and never wondered about anything.

The most amazing sound he heard was from the angels' wings. They produced a beautiful, holy melody of never-ending praise.

The most vivid memory he has of heaven was the melodies of praise that was nonstop and intense. The endless variety amazed him.

As he approached the large gate, he heard the praise music from every direction, comprised of melodies and tones he had never experienced.

He heard lots of "Hallelujah!" "Praise!" "Glory to God!" "Praise to the King!"[2]

All the sounds blended, and each voice or instrument enhanced the others. Don heard many of the choruses and hymns he had sung at various times along with hundreds of songs he had never heard before.

His heart was filled with the deepest joy and peace.

The wall faded out of sight in both directions—and at the top. Don could not see the top or the walls going in either direction.

The gate glowed and shimmered.

Seeing inside the gate, he saw a city with paved streets of gold. He was thrilled to be able to go in. The crowd joined beside him as he was ready to enter through the gate.

He realized he had become part of the choir. He lingered to gaze for a brief time. Then, suddenly, he left the gates.

TWENTY-ONE

Choo Thomas

CHOO THOMAS (1939-2013) WAS an author and minister who experienced supernatural encounters with the Lord Jesus Christ during her adult life. Thomas was a Korean American living in Washington State, USA, after growing up in Korea.

While Choo's parents were not of the Christian faith, she herself became a follower of Jesus Christ in 1992 and went on to be a dedicated servant of the Lord. Thomas was married and had two children as well as grandchildren.

In 1996, Jesus began visiting Choo and giving her visions. These experiences would often happen in the middle of the night, in the early morning hours.

The typical vision would begin with them on a beach walking. They would then go to heaven, change into heavenly clothing, cross over a golden bridge, and begin a journey through parts of heaven.

Much of Jesus and Choo's conversations were about the heavenly realm, nature, the beautiful aspects of heaven, the work that Choo was to do for the Lord, Jesus' return, and the importance of having a pure heart and love for the Lord above all other loves.

Early during the experiences, Jesus showed Choo graphic visions of hell, with people burning in a sea of blood. Choo even saw her own parents in hell.

After the vision of hell, Jesus took her to a place she calls "animal mountain," a paradise where animals live in harmony (Isaiah 65:24-25).[1]

They then went back to the waterside where they visited shiny mansions and castles on streets of gold. They entered a castle, which had an indescribable beauty inside. The walls were made of multicolored precious gems. She went upstairs.

Jesus introduced her to Abraham, who had long white hair and a flowing beard. He called over an angel to escort Choo.

Thomas was still sad about her parents being lost in hell. Jesus sensed her sadness and comforted her, telling her he wished none of His children had to go there.
He emphasized the importance of obedience and purity in a person's walk with Him.

Jesus emphasized His urgency regarding His return. He also continued to emphasize Choo's calling, work, and special anointing. Since Choo was so disturbed about her parents being in hell, Jesus touched her eyes and removed the memory of seeing her mother's face in hell.

On March 4, the Lord took Choo to heaven, where they went into a white building. Jesus showed her a group of men wearing gowns and crowns and a big black Bible. They crossed the golden bridge and walked along a hillside next to a beautiful valley. They both picked and ate some purple fruit from one of the trees.

Jesus called the area "a place of living water."[2] He drank some of it and gave some to Choo. It was the most delicious, sweetest water she had ever tasted.

He then took her to her mansion, a place prepared just for her. She explored the house, as she cried tears of joy and gratitude and sang songs.

They returned to the golden bridge, and Jesus talked about His return, the urgency of it, and the work He had for her to do.

Thomas' supernatural experiences continued, so much so that she became exhausted, with her body feeling the physical effects.

Again Jesus took her on a journey. They visited the white building and a powder room. Choo saw men who Jesus said wrote the Bible. Before them was a black Bible radiating with the power of the Holy Spirit.

They walked through a verdant valley near the crystal river. They visited her house again. Jesus continued to talk about her work for Him and the fact that He would enable and empower her to do it.

He told her this would be the last time He would take her to the kingdom. "My daughter, I have shown you enough for a while . . . I know how tired you are right now . . . You must rest for a while."[3]

Later, Jesus and Choo, standing on a mountain, flew down to a fertile valley with pure white streets and white houses. Jesus showed her a beautiful house. They walked some more before they ascended straight up like a helicopter rises. They returned to the same mountain they were on, where they went to a pond.

At the pond, Jesus explained important things about this particular journey, such as telling her that the houses they saw are in Jerusalem—the Holy City. He also encouraged her regarding the work Jesus had called her to complete.

Choo realized she had walked in the New Jerusalem, where only the pure in heart will be allowed (Revelation 21:25-27). She realized that she had tasted water from the river of life, walked down the streets, seen the trees, and tasted the fruit (Revelation 22:1-2).

Jesus had given her the same message He gave to John: "Behold, I am coming quickly! Blessed is he who keeps the words of the prophecy of this book" (Revelation

22:7).[4]

Jesus continued to visit Thomas and give her visions.

Jesus directly told Choo that "even faithful Christians doubt that there really is a kingdom of heaven. I want all of My doubting children to believe My kingdom is real."[5]

TWENTY-TWO

Maurice Maelo

MAURICE MAELO IS a bishop, pastor, and minister in Durban, South Africa, a tropical port city of 3.5 million people on the east coast of South Africa. Maelo is a Durban native and comes from a large family.

Maelo has ministered in many countries during his career. He was trained as a minister in Nairobi, Kenya.

It was in Nairobi in 1995 that Maurice and one of his brothers were in a horrific, tragic car accident. Maurice actually died and experienced heaven but came back to life on earth.

On March 29, 1995, Maelo was with about 15 other people traveling in a taxi on the busy streets of Nairobi, a bustling commercial city of 3.3 million people. The taxi was hit twice on the street, resulting in the death of basically everyone in the taxi except the Maelo brothers.

Maurice was declared dead and was actually grouped with the other deceased. His mother and brother prayed fervently for him to live.

While dead, his spirit visited heaven, where he saw the glories of heaven, spent time with Jesus, and was commissioned before he came back to earth.

Immediately after the wreck, Maurice landed in the "corridors of heaven," almost like the a sparrow might land.1 The presence and light of God were evident. There was a feeling of calm.

People were standing completely silent in a line. Their faces were full of fear and uncertainty. Every few seconds, more people would join the line.

Maurice could see a majestic being standing at the other end of the line. This being was a heavenly general and was tall with broad shoulders. His body language, face, and eyes were full of discernment. Maelo felt so small in his presence. Any secret deeds or actions were exposed to this being.

These feelings caused every person to have fear about where their spirit would be sent.

The general was shouting three different words with a piercing voice of authority: depart, enter, or return.

For every person in the growing line, it was a final moment. When the being said "depart," with power and volume, that person was being denied heaven.

Maurice could tell people were stressed: they were pale, sorrowful, and uncertain. It felt like facing an impartial judge who simply tells you "right" or "wrong," and your fate is sealed, with no questions, arguments, or discussion.[2]

Maurice could hear the screams of people who were told to "depart," as they passed through the corridors heading to hell. The screams were of total agony. It was scary.

Soon there were six people ahead of Maurice. Three of them were told to depart, while the fourth was told to "enter." The general's voice was like thunder.

The person allowed in had joy on his face, with hands uplifted. The gates were opened for him. Angels received him quickly, leading him into heaven. Songs of joy were sung.

One woman in front of him was deceived and did not see her nakedness. She had been dancing and saying "hallelujah!"[3] She was told to depart. She screamed bitterly, her face turned red, and she was escorted out. Her screams were heard down the corridors.

Maurice was very concerned. Who could make it? The general said, "And you!" Maurice was in fear. It was the moment of truth.

"And you, what you were given to do you haven't even finished, and what are you doing here?" the general said.[4]

For some time he was speechless. The statement created electric waves of echo in the corridors. Maurice wanted to say something, to defend himself, but he was not quick enough. The general shouted, "Return!"[5]

In the blink of an eye, Maurice was back in his body.

Maelo was then in a coma in the hospital for 10 days. He could hear what was going on in his room. At one point, while a believer was visiting his room, severe pain entered Maurice's body. His spirit left, and he was immediately in heaven.

He found himself standing on a street of gold, surrounded by the most fabulous gardens he had ever seen. A river of crystal clear waters flowed north of the garden.

The lawns were perfect, and the flowers were in bloom. Springs of water spinkled the entire gardens. The gold on the streets was pure and transparent. Everything was still and calm.

An angel was close by on his right. Maurice was standing with his left hand across his chest and his right hand on his cheek. He looked and saw that the angel was standing in just the same way. The angel walked toward Maurice, as if to begin to show him around and tell him why he was there.

They took just two steps, and they were out of the gardens and at the sea of glass, a mind-blowing experience. The sea is like crystal clear glass (Revelation 4:1-8).

The throne of God is on the sea of glass. At the throne, Maurice was overwhelmed with indescribable feelings, in awe that he was able to stand at the feet of the Father God.

Repeatedly, the 24 elders laid their crowns down before the throne and prostrated themselves, stood up, and raised their hands up to God. Watching this, Maurice wanted to worship as well. When he tried, he fell to the floor, the presence of God overwhelming him (Revelation 4:10).[6]

From Maelo's experience, heaven is created to worship God. Maelo writes:

"The One who sits on the throne is awesome and fearful in his praises; no one is like Him. Where shall we go if we disobey His word and defy His authority?"[7]

As he worshipped in awe on the floor, the angel stood motionless and watched him for a time. The angel then picked up Maurice respectfully and easily, using just one hand, as if to say "you have seen enough."[8]

Maelo's amazing revelation is that angels are like our nurses, both in heaven and on earth, 24 hours a day non-stop.

Whenever the angel led him, the angel took Maurice's right hand. The angels seemed to act on command, with much order.

After a while, the angel of the Lord took Maurice's hand, took a few steps, and they were back on the golden streets. The big and majestic angel stepped back a few steps. Out of the corner of Maurice's eye, he saw someone a little distance away. He was amazed. It was the Lord Jesus.

Jesus face south of the garden, holding His hands behind Him, in a very restful manner.

From a distance, Maurice could not mistake his gentle posture, his authority, and His sense of ownership. Maurice feels that Jesus is not just gentle—He is gentleness itself. A person just knows it.

To Maelo, Jesus looked humble and gentle, yet He owns both heaven, earth, and everything in them. Jesus was settled and calm, taking a keen interest in every person.

Maurice feels like it was a most outstanding act of love by Jesus that He would take time to wait for Maurice and spend substantial time with him.

Jesus was between six and seven feet tall. He was dressed in a white robe down to His feet, with a golden sash around His chest. There was a golden rope around his waist. He wore leather-like sandals on his feet.

TWENTY-FOUR

Bill Smith

WILLIAM "BILL" SMITH is a songwriter and musician who experienced heaven. Smith always had a deep desire to know God, being that he himself was adopted as a child.

One day, Smith was lying on his bed and praying, when suddenly the ceiling disappeared. He saw only swirling clouds of splendor and glory in fiery colors. He heard a loud sound with extreme power. Fearful, trembling, and terrified, he saw a large cloud coming toward him. He was in a spiritual dimension, in the spirit realm.

He saw his body consumed in fire. The loud cosmic sounds were so terrifying he thought he might die. At the same time, he heard a song he had written to the Lord, "Run, Run into the Son."

The cloud of fire went to his feet and went up, continuing up his legs, torso, chest, throat, and arms. A voice spoke to him, "This is death."[1] Yet he had no fear, no physical reaction. He died.

The Holy Spirit was in control. Bill had no confusion. He realized he was still alive on the other side, so he had peace. All he wanted was the Father and Jesus.

He moved upward, to a higher place. He realized he was

moving into God. Later, he realized that he "had escaped the imprisonment of the [the] soul and was free to be part of what was outside [himself] in the spiritual realm."[2] Bill writes: "You have no idea in this life on earth how much God is all over and around you all the time. He's always there."

He saw the heavens open and saw the wheels that Ezekial saw (Ezekiel 1:16). He saw a massive array of wheels and lights, full of splendor, glory, flames of fire, and millions of colors he had never seen. It all move in explosiveness.

At first, the wheels did not make sense to Bob. On one level, the wheel contains multiple personalities, angels, and people. Moreover, he realized that the wheels are related to the spinning of the universe. The many aspects of the Almighty God are involved, such as His truth, His majesty, His wonder, His power, and so forth. They all work together and create a symphony of celestial music with majestic harmony.[3]

His eyes were gleaming and welcoming. His hair was white as snow, thick, and hanging down below His shoulders and onto His back. His face "oozed with love" that was tangible and real, one could see it.[9]

In Jesus' eyes, there was a mixture of kindness, mercy, and understanding. His compassion and love together assured Maurice that Jesus understands him better than anyone else ever would. His face is radiant and inviting.

Jesus held Maurice close, holding him tenderly. He looked into Maurice's eyes intently and compassionately. Maurice cried, and Jesus stroked the side of his face with two thumbs. Then, Jesus dried his tears and said "It is all right."[10]

Then they took a walk, hand in hand, through the gardens and on the golden streets.

North of the garden, there was crystal clear water flowing. Jesus let Maurice check the area out, not hurrying him at all. They looked at the flowers there, smiling at each other.

Suddenly Jesus stopped. He tapped Maurice on the shoulder, bent down to him, and said, "Go back and tell them, I am coming back soon!"[11]

Their meeting was over, and Maurice felt a tremendous loneliness as Jesus departed.

TWENTY-THREE

Khalida Wukawitz

KHALIDA WUKAWITZ IS a Palestinian woman with a Muslim background who now lives in the USA.

In a life filled with great difficulty and seemingly impossible circumstances and situations, Khalida eventually made it out of both a nomadic tribal life in Arab countries and am abusive marriage which kept her secluded and in fear.

An orphan in Palestine, Khalida was found as a child, sold into slavery to a Bedouin family. For years she was part of a caravan that traveled from country to country seeking survival. After getting married, she and her husband moved to the USA, where she met a Christian woman and was able to escape the marriage. Today, she ministers to and helps others.

The Christian woman offered her a job and a home for Khalida and her children. For two years, the woman shared her faith with Khalida, who was a devout Muslim and was sure Islam was the only true faith. She was raised with the Qur'an and loved Mohammed.[1]

Realizing she was very unhappy and that "nothing was working," Khalida asked Jesus, "if you are the Son of God, come down and show me."[2]

Something happened. Suddenly, a person was standing in front of her. He spoke to her in Arabic, saying "I am the truth, the life, and the way, and no one comes to the Father except by Me."[3]

She knew immediately it was Jesus. His voice was like rushing waters. Jesus was glorious and beautiful. He was light inside of Light.

She told Him he was Lord. He responded, "Yes, I am Jesus, the One you denied . . . I came to save you, to make you a happy person . . . Believe in Me."[4]

Jesus got so close to her that there was too much light for her to see His eyes. Somehow, light came with His being. As He was there, Khalida became part of heaven.

Jesus said, "You are My daughter." The words were like living water. Being in His presence, she realized that she was His and that through the blood of Jesus she was forgiven.[5]

Then, she saw three men. With Jesus on her right, the three men were surrounded by light. The oldest man was wearing a royal robe and had a long beard. Jesus told her they were Abraham, Isaac, and Jacob. He said (without words), "Go to the bosom of your Father Abraham." She did, and Abraham welcomed her. Jesus told her to repent from the curse words they used to curse the Jewish people.[6]

Khalida was in heaven. There were no language barriers. Angels cried "Holy, holy, holy." She saw a large crown that people threw at the feet of Jesus. She saw children worshipping Jesus, who explained these were children who died through abortion, murder, or sickness.

There were multitudes of people, millions of people worshiping Jesus the Lord, calling him "Holy, Holy Lamb of God" over and over. She saw crystal clear water. She saw angels, babies, and birds at Jesus' feet. The Spirit of God revealed it all to her.

Khalida was worshiping and calling Him "My God, my

Savior, and my King," feeling all of this in her body, when heaven began facing away slowly. She started to sense she was back on the earth.[7]

She begged Jesus not to leave. He replied in Arabic, "I'm going to come back and get you."[8] He put His hand on her before He left. She lay flat on the floor, and heaven faded away. She began to speak in a language she had heard in heaven, feeling strength inside of her. She was filled with the power of Jesus. She felt healed from her pain. There was a change in her heart. She felt freedom and love.

TWENTY-FIVE

Mary Neal

Dr. Mary Neal is an orthopedic surgeon based in Jackson Hole, Wyoming, USA. In 1999, while on a trip to Chile in South America, Mary experienced heaven.

Mary and her husband Bill and their four children enjoy outdoor activities including boating and paddling. Mary and Bill went to Chile to enjoy the culture and the outdoors, especially kayaking. They are both experienced kayakers.

Mary was with a group of friends kayaking the Fuy River, one of Chile's well-known white water boating and paddling rivers, with several waterfalls and many levels of rapids. Bill did not go that day due to an injury.

While cascading down a waterfall of 10 to 20 feet, Mary was pinned under water. While struggling to save herself, she "asked for God's will be done."[1] She did not ask to be saved but just that His will be done.

Suddenly, she was "overcome with a very physical sensation of being held, comforted, and reassured."[2] Mary was "overcome with an absolute feeling of calm, peace, and of the very physical sensation of being help in someone's arms while being stroked and comforted . . ."[3] At the same time, she also felt a certainty that everything would be okay, no matter what the outcome would be. Mary assumed she would die and wanted to "get on with the journey, whatever that was meant to be."[4]

Members of her group, some of whom were friends who are trained in water rescue, tried desperately to rescue Mary, with no success. After several minutes, they felt a supernatural change and were able to somehow dislodge the boat from it's stuck location. Mary floated downstream and was rescued and placed on shore. Her friends performed CPR, prayed, called out to Mary again and again, and somehow, Mary began taking breaths and finally breathing.

During her drowning ordeal, Mary was fully aware of what was happening but did not feel pain and surprisingly felt great. Though she knew she was dying, she actually "felt better than I've ever felt."[5] At the moment her body was released and she began to tumble down the river, she felt a "pop."[6]

She felt as if she had gotten rid of her old self, feeing her soul. She rose up out of the water and was met by a group of 15 to 20 souls who were very happy to see her. She was also happy to see them and knew that they had known her her entire life. Mary compares them to the great cloud of witnesses (Hebrews 12:1).

The people had been sent to guide her across the "divide of time and dimension that separates our world from God's."[7]

These spiritual beings were dazzling and radiant, with edges blurred. Their presence filled and consumed her senses. Mary and the souls communicated purely, through thoughts and emotions. They understood each other without using words.

The group joyously celebrated Mary's arrival, and "absolute love was palpable" as they hugged, danced, and greeted each other.[8] Mary's feelings and sensations cannot be described in words.

"It's impossible for me to adequately describe what I saw and what I felt...The appropriate words, descriptions, and concepts don't even exist in our current language.[9]

Soon Mary and her companions were gliding down a brilliant path, and she saw a large domed structure that was exploding with beauty and color and the love of God, beyond what she can describe or explain.

She felt her soul being pulled toward the structure. She was absorbed in its radiance and felt complete and pure unconditional love emanating from the hall.

To Mary, it was the most beautiful and alluring thing she had ever seen or experienced.

Mary felt sure this hall is the "gate through which each human being must pass" and the place where we review our lives and choices.[10]

Mary had a deep sensation that she was home. But suddenly, she also felt disappointment, as she knew it was not her time to stay. She and her companions knew that she still had work to do on earth.

Mary did not want to leave and protested. She then began to see her body on the riverbank. The people returned Mary there, and she was reunited with her body.

Dr. Neal's friends and husband transported her to receive care, first in Chile and then back to her home in Wyoming.

TWENTY-SIX

David Taylor

DAVID TAYLOR IS an apostle and minister based in St. Louis, Missouri, USA. He serves in the fivefold ministry offices which in addition to apostle include prophet, pastor, evangelist, and teacher. David has experienced numerous supernatural encounters with Jesus Christ. In 2000 at the age of 27, Taylor was taken to heaven.

Suddenly, he was standing in front of Jesus, who had a pleasant smile on His face. Jesus did not talk but took David to talk to various people. These talks would serve as the foundation, catalyst, and confirmation of Taylor's life and ministry.

They approached two men. The first was an evangelist Taylor did not know. The second was the evangelist Smith Wigglesworth, who spoke to Taylor about Taylor's ministry. Smith pointed out that David had lost power due to his lack of consecration. The crowds and attendance at his meetings had decreased, because he had not paid the price for the anointing and power of God.

Smith told David to return to earth and study the great men and women that God called and used in significant ways.

Then, David saw the preacher Kathryn Kuhlman who was walking over a beautiful golden bridge. After running to catch up to her, he asked her how she got the Lord into her life in such a powerful way.

"Don't stop preaching the word of God and, furthermore, don't desecrate!" Kuhlman replied.[1] The word "desecrate" means "to disrespect holy things."

Taylor took this to mean, in addition to keeping the word of God first and foremost, that when a person dies to self, they should not mourn their death or spiritually defiled. A key is to stay dead to self.[2]

He then fellowshipped with Bishop C.H. Mason, the founder of the pentecostal denomination Church of God in Christ. Mason talked about the Holy Spirit coming upon him while he was on earth and about dancing in the spirit. He encouraged Taylor to go back to dancing in the spirit. When Mason danced right there, glory filled the place they were in. Taylor realized that miracles occurred when Mason would dance on earth.

Taylor was surprised that saints and angels in heaven seemed to know him already, though he had never met them. Jesus answered: "Everyone here knows you because I have spoken of you to them."[3] Jesus then referenced his words in Matthew 10:32: "Therefore whoever confesses Me before men, I will also confess before My Father who is in heaven."[4]

Just briefly, Taylor caught a glimpse of Mount Zion, the city of God. Its landscape was on a slope but was not necessarily a high mountain as some think it is.

He and many others were walking up toward the highest point where the Father was sitting. All the people had on beautiful white robes. He saw the beautiful, golden walls surrounding the city. David could see through the walls.

In 1992, Taylor, then 19, was taken to heaven in a dream. He was permitted to go inside one room that was filled with massive books that had everyone's life written down inside the books. The books were like giant, family-sized coffee table books. They were white and gold.

Taylor saw his own book, titled "God's Plan." Inside, everything he was ordained to do was written. The book was blank on the right side, which would be filled in with the choices Taylor would make in his life (see Psalm 69:28, 139:16, 56:8).

Jesus then revealed to Taylor a truth and mystery. He said to David: "I've come to reveal two great mysteries to you and to my church."[5]

Taylor saw a screen displaying one of his services. He was preaching, pacing back and forth and then walking off the stage. When he walked off, he saw the Jesus was preaching where David was before.

Jesus said, "I've come to tell you and My church the mystery of Christ in you—the hope of glory for the world . . . When you ask me to come take over your body and mouth, I do this before you minister."[6] Then He said another truth: "I dwell inside of you; I walk in you."[7] Jesus explained that He will walk in and dwell inside peoples' bodies, for their bodies are His temple.

Jesus then revealed to Taylor that Jesus would work with Taylor personally and heal people in his services. He told Taylor He brought him to heaven "to build up and encourage confidence, in you and in My people."[8] Taylor confirmed that he saw Jesus do miracles and healings in his services.

Next they passed by the 24 elders around the Throne. Taylor wondered why God would need elders, when God knows everything. Jesus answered and explained that "purposes are established in the multitude of counselors."[9] Jesus explained that He lives His own word (such as Proverbs 15:22, the "multitude of counselors") and that the elders "advise us (the Father and Son) concerning My word and what We have already said."[10]

David got to experience the Father's Throne. He was taken into a big room with glory all around. The power in the room was so overwhelming that he could not stand up but was quickly on his face. The light was so brilliant he could not see. He raised his head enough to view God's feet. David's body had no strength.

Amazingly, David was able to see God's arms and hands resting on the Throne's armrests. The Father was wearing a beautiful, gold wedding band. Jesus explained to Taylor that He and the Father are betrothed in marriage to David.

Jesus explained the different relationship levels of believers, including: friendship, sonship, servanthood, stewardship, kingship, and the marriage relationship.

Scriptures about God entering into a marriage covenent with His people include 1 Corinthians 6:17, Hosea 2:19-20, and Isaiah 54:5. 173 If someone is married to the Lord, they are in a more committed relationship with Him.

Walking to the edge of heaven, they were about to part ways. Jesus had a great smile on His face as He said these final words to Taylor: "Have intercessors pray for you."[11]

Jesus waved goodbye, and David was taken back to earth and was back in his body.

TWENTY-SEVEN

Michael McCormack

Michael McCormack, son of Ian McCormack, was ten years old when he saw heaven in a vision.

Sitting in church, a light shone on him. He was lifted into the heavens, as angels in white robes and with wings surrounded him and hovered over him.

Arriving at heaven's gate, which is golden, Michael could see a massive palace and a town with a wall around it. Suddenly Jesus was next to him. He was wearing white, shining clothing. His eyes were kind. The Lord took him through lovely meadows with rabbits, deer, and foxes.

Jesus took him to the Throne Room of God. There were lights, pillars, and jewels everywhere. There were two rows of angels with golden trumpets. There were big angels with white robes and wings. Their faces were like men's faces.

There was noise from the trumpeting, the angels' singing, and the angels' playing of instruments, including harps and something similar to a tambourine. There were creatures which were combinations of different animals, such as a lion with eagle's wings on its back.

Jesus held out a wooden staff, like a shepherd's staff, and pointed. Michael saw three thrones that were somehow joined together, symbolizing the Trinity. The thrones were golden, with rainbow-colored jewels covering them. The jewels were emeralds, rubies, sapphires, yellow and purple stones, and more.

Angels were dancing in bright, colorful clouds, and Michael joined them.

Jesus and Michael visited the town, which had golden roads, houses, and the River of Life, crystal clear and moving fast. The Tree of Life was at the mouth of the River and had lots of fruit on it. Michael knew that children would pick fruit each day for their family from the tree.

Near the River, Jesus cupped his hands, dipped them in the River, and anointed Michael with the water. Michael felt power flowing into him.

Then they went to a door made from an oak tree. Michael opened the door, seeing a beautiful garden filled with wildlife, lakes, waterfalls, rainbows, and many deer drinking from a lake. It was a beautiful scene with a lovely aroma. Jesus said, "This is the New Earth that we will treasure."[1]

Jesus showed Michael the old earth, which was grey and dull and covered with a black mist, which was sin. Jesus was sad. They visited it, seeing that there was no life. Jesus said, "This is the earth that man has destroyed. What I have shown you I want more people to see. I have shown you this because I want you to tell the people that you have seen this and that they should turn back to God. This is what is going to happen and you can't stop this . . . but you can help save more people."[2]

Jesus left, and Michael woke up in the church.[3]

TWENTY-EIGHT

Colton Burpo

COLTON BURPO IS a young minister and speaker and the subject of the hit book and movie, *Heaven is For Real*. He and his parents are the founders of Heaven is For Real Ministries (heavenlive.org).

Published in 2010, *Heaven is For Real* has been a top bestseller and is a major motion picture (Paramount, 2014).

In 2003, Colton, two months away from his fourth birthday, experienced the glories of heaven for a short time. During the next few years, he revealed his experiences to his parents, Sonja and Todd, and to others.

In heaven, he spent time with Jesus, saw angels and people, spoke to John the Baptist, spoke to his great grandfather, saw God's throne, and more.

The book, written by Colton's father, recounts the Burpo family's interaction with Colton as, over time, he reveals to them his amazing experiences. The family of four live in Nebraska, USA, where father Todd is a pastor and small business owner.

In February 2003, young Colton faced a very serious

burst appendix and emergency appendectomy and spent about 15 days in the hospital. His parents cried out to God, and friends and church members prayed for his healing.

During the next several months and even years, Colton's family would eventually find out that Colton visited heaven. The book is a stirring account of Colton's parents' amazement and wonder at their son's supernatural experience and resulting spiritual knowledge and understanding.

Months after the health scare, the family was driving on a short trip when Todd and wife Sonja asked Colton about his hospital stay. Sonja asked Colton is he remembered the hospital. Colton replied that he did and that it was where the angels sang to him

Todd asked him what the angels sang to him. Colton responded: "They sang 'Jesus Loves Me' and 'Joshua Fought the Battle of Jericho.'"

"What did the angels looks like?"

"Well, one of them looked like Grandpa Dennis, but it wasn't him, 'cause Grandpa Dennis has glasses." Then Colton grew serious, "Dad, Jesus had the angels sing to me because I was scared. They made me feel better .. I was sitting in Jesus' lap."[1]

Colton confirmed this happened while he was in the hospital, explaining that dad Todd was praying and mom Sonja was talking on the phone. Todd asked him how Colton could know where his parents were. Colton spoke matter-of-factly:

"Cause I could see you. I went up out of my body and I was looking down and I could see the doctor working on my body. And I saw you and mommy. You were in a little room by yourself, praying; and Mommy was in a different room, and she was praying and talking on the phone.'"[2]

After the surgery and recovery, Colton was back to his normal self. When the family faced the medical bills, he said, "Dad, Jesus used Dr. O'Holleran to fix me . . . You should pay him."[3]

When Todd was preparing to preside over a funeral, Colton asked if the deceased had Jesus in his heart. Colton was insistent, "He had to have Jesus in his heart! He had to know Jesus or he can't get into heaven!"[4]

Later, Todd felt like it was the right time to discuss now four-year-old Colton's experience, making sure to ask open-ended questions and not give his son any help. Todd asked, "Remember when . . . you talked about sitting on Jesus' lap? . . . Well, did anything else happen?"

Colton nodded, and his eyes were bright. "Did you know that Jesus has a cousin? Jesus told me his cousin baptized him. . . . I don't remember his name, but he was nice."[5]

Then Colton spotted a plastic horse among his toys. He told his dad that he got to pet Jesus' "rainbow horse" and told Todd "There's lots of colors."[6]

"Hey, Dad, did you know Jesus has a horse?"

Todd was truly amazed.

Later that evening, Todd asked Colton what Jesus looked like. Colton responded that Jesus has "markers."[7]
Todd did not understand what Colton meant.

"Markers, Daddy . . . Jesus has markers. And he has brown hair and he has hair on his face . . . And his eyes . . . oh, Dad, his eyes are so pretty!"[8] Todd realized Colton did not know the word beard.

As he said this, Colton's seemed to enjoy thinking of the memory.

"What about his clothes?"

"He had purple on." As he said this, Colton put his hand on his left shoulder, moved it across his body down to his right hip then repeated the motion. "His clothes were white, but it was purple from here to here." Colton also did not know the word sash.[9]

Colton explained that Jesus was the only person in heaven with purple on. He also described Jesus' crown. Then, he stood and pointed out Jesus' "markers," by pointing to the palms of his right hand and left hand and the tops of his feet.

"That's where Jesus' markers are, Daddy," Colton told his dad.[10]

Todd realized that Colton had to have learned this in

heaven. The gruesome facts of the crucifixion had likely never been explained to Colton.

Some time later, Todd asked Colton what he did in heaven.

"Homework," Colton smiled. "Jesus was my teacher . . . Jesus gave me work to do, and that was my favorite part of heaven. There were lots of kids, Dad."[11]

Over the next year or so, Colton named a lot of the kids he said were in heaven with him. He explained that "everybody's got wings" and that his own wings were not very big.[12]

Colton explained that Jesus went up and down "like an elevator" while everyone else flew. People had light above their heads, wore white robe-like garments, and had yellow sashes across their chests. Angels wore different colors.

He told his dad he died, "just for a little bit," was gone for three minutes.[13]

As time went on, Colton revealed more and more about his trip to heaven. He said Jesus told him he had to go back to earth because Jesus was answering Todd's prayer. Colton told Todd about spending time in heaven with Pop, Todd's maternal grandfather who passed away 23 years before Colton was born. He told Todd that Jesus was happy when Todd decided to become a pastor.

He also told Todd about meeting the Burpo's "other daughter," the child they lost to a miscarriage.[14] God had adopted her. She was very excited to see Colton and about the prospect and meeting her parents later.

One evening, after Todd asked Colton if he had seen God's throne, Colton said he had seen it numerous times. Colton went on to explain how big God is, how much He loves mankind, that Jesus' chair is next to his Dad's, that the Holy Spirit is blue in color, and that God and Jesus provide the light for heaven.[15]

One night while reading a story to his son, Todd asked Colton if he had seen God's throne.

"Oh, yeah! I saw that a bunch of times! It was big, Dad . . . really, really big, because God is the biggest one there is.

And he really, really loves us, Dad. You can't belieeeeve how much he loves us!"

"And do you know that Jesus sits right next to God! Jesus' chair is right next to his Dad's."

Colton said he was given a little chair and sat next to the Holy Spirit.

"I was sitting by God the Holy Spirit because I was praying for you. You needed the Holy Spirit, so I prayed for you."

"What does God look like? God the Holy Spirit?" Todd asked

"Hmm, that's kind of a hard one . . . he's kind of blue."

Colton also said, "God and Jesus light up heaven. It never gets dark. It's always bright."[16]

Colton saw the gates of heaven, the heavenly city, and animals of every kind. He talked often about how Jesus loves the children as well as about the magnificent colors in heaven.

Near Easter, Colton explained that Jesus told him He had to die on their cross so that people on earth could go see his Dad.

When discussing with his sister the idea to pray for their Dad's preaching, Colton said that Jesus shoots down power for Todd when Todd is talking.

After watching a movie as a family, Colton explained that "There are too swords in heaven! . . . Mom, Satan's not in hell yet . . . The angels carry swords so they can keep Satan out of heaven!"[17]

With Colton talking about the dark side, Todd asked if he had seen Satan during his supernatural experience. Any time Satan was brought up, Colton changed completely in negative ways and stopped talking. He had apparently seen something unpleasant and didn't want to talk about it.

Amazingly, Colton also talked about the coming apocalyptal events, explaining that he had seen the war that would destroy the world, as Jesus, the angels, and the good people fight against Satan, monsters, and bad people. The men would fight with Jesus while the women and children watched. Jesus would win and throw Satan into hell.[18]

TWENTY-NINE

Dean Braxton

DEAN BRAXTON IS a minister and founder of Dean Braxton Ministries in Tacoma, Washington, USA, near Seattle. He and wife Marilyn have six children.

In May 2006, Braxton had a near death experience and visited heaven.

At the time, Dean worked in the Juvenile Justice System in King County, Seattle, as a Supervisor of two Courts. Dean is originally from California. Though he did not grow up in a Christian family, today many in his extended family are Christians.

On a work day, Dean was in pain and went to the hospital with kidney stones and a high fever. His condition quickly deteriorated, and his heart stopped. He was in the hospital for 13 days, nine days in intensive care, and actually died for 1 hour and 45 minutes.

During his crisis, Marilyn interceded and mobilized a prayer chain and network that ultimately helped save Dean's life. He was miraculously healed of 29 different conditions. While facing death, he came before Jesus three times. Since then, Braxton shares his testimony as part of his ministry.

While in the hospital, Dean knew he was headed to Jesus. In the blink of an eye, he was immediately in the Lord's presence. The prayers of many people passed him by as he traveled to heaven.

The first place he went was to the feet of Jesus. All he could say was "Thank you, thank you, thank you . . ."[1] He knew that the reason he was there was because of Jesus. Everything about Dean praised Him.

In heaven, there was continual praise and worship. More than just hearing it, Dean experienced it.

As he knelt before Jesus, it was pure joy. Jesus was pure light, brighter than the noonday sun. To Dean, it seemed that if someone was not right with God, they would be burned up in Jesus' presence.

Braxton: "Jesus is more beautiful, wonderful, and glorious that I can explain . . . How do I tell you what His face looks like? His face was as if it were liquid crystal glass made up of pure love, light, and life."[2]

Dean describes how the colors of the rainbow and indescribable colors came from His face. However, it was not that Jesus was the colors. Dean was seeing the colors and was part of the colors. Dean was seeing Jesus and was part of Jesus. He was in Jesus, who was shining out of Dean.

Dean received a supernatural revelation of Jesus' love. He realized that Jesus has divine love for each and every individual on earth.[3]

He saw parts of Jesus' body. Jesus still has the wounds in his feet from the piercing of them. His hands still had the nail piercings. Dean realized what Jesus' went through for us, how much it cost in pain to His physical body for us to be redeemed. Jesus still bears the scars of His suffering.

He wore a crown that looked like the sun, shooting off rays.

His head and hair were white like wool, as white as snow.

Jesus' eyes were like flames of fire with changing colors. They were deep and full of life. It was like Jesus had love for Dean—and for every other individual person. That love was in His eyes. Dean saw in Jesus eyes' that Jesus wants every person on earth to be in heaven eventually. He does not want anyone to go to hell.[4]

Dean realized that heaven is massive and expanding. Things seemed far yet near. If he wanted to be somewhere, all he had to do was think it.

Heaven is bright from the glory of God. The Father and the Son's light shines out of everything. The atmosphere was something you experienced.

Jesus' words are alive, and His voice was mighty and full of love.

Communication in heaven was generally through thought and was something "experienced," not just heard.

Dean writes, "There was a rule that you did not go into any other's thoughts without them giving you permission to do so."[5]

Worship was such a part of heaven that it was like breathing on the earth. In heaven, every living being and creature—even every part of God's creation—praises the Father and Jesus.

The flowers, birds, water, mountains, and everything praised the Lord.

Moreover, Dean received a revelation that everything in heaven is connected as well.

While going to and from heaven, Braxton literally saw prayers traveling faster than he was.[6]

A type of prayer he saw was prayers from people who knew the authority they had, who were praying by faith. The prayers went straight to the throne and the Father.

Dean's revelation about the throne is this: the throne of God is not a seat. It is a place, but even more than that. God the Father Himself is the throne. Dean came to realize that God answers our prayers with Himself. And he hears prayers from the heart. He hears and understands our hearts.

Braxton saw Jesus strategizing. He pointed to a place in an earthly city and gave an angel an assignment. Jesus received the prayer about a situation and passed information to the angels.

Jesus told Dean to emphasize to those on earth that believers on earth are just passing through.

God the Father

Dean attempts to describe the Father God, though he admits he has no words or thoughts sufficient for it.

God the Father is Spirit, pure Spirit. He is pure Love, Life, and Light. He is vast, infinite, immeasurable, never-ending, endless, and without end. We are made in His image.

He is sitting on the throne, yet He is the throne! There is an immeasurable number of heavenly creatures before the throne giving God praise.

It was hard for Dean to take in everything he experienced at the throne. What really stood out was the love the Father has for all of us on earth. God has specific love for every individual person. The very air we breath is from God.

In heaven, the Father and Jesus live outside of every being and inside every being.

Between the beings around the throne and the throne, there was something like water, like a crystal sea. After the sea, there was another liquid under the throne of God. This liquid had a different density from the sea. These two liquids flowed through each other but did not blend together. In heaven there are other "liquids" that are alive and delightful.[7]

Braxton had another revelation. As he worshipped and saw praise and worship, he realized that God the Father actually sings back to His people, individually. He sang a pure song of love from His Spirit to the one it was meant for.

Furthermore, God is sending these love songs to people on earth, and nothing can stop it.

THIRTY

Marvin Besteman

MARVIN BESTEMAN (1935-2012) was a banker and financial industry executive in Grand Rapids, Michigan, USA. Marvin and his wife Ruth had three children.

In 2006, Marvin Besteman, 71, experienced a life-changing preview of eternity, visiting heaven's gate for about half an hour. At the time, Besteman was in the hospital and in severe pain, having just had surgery to remove a pancreatic tumor. After his experience, he was very hesitant to share his story, as he felt like people would not believe him.

In the middle of night on April 28, 2006, while on his hospital bed, suddenly two men walked into Marvin's room.1 He knew they were angels. They were about 5'8" to 5'10", one having longish brown hair, the other shorter hair.

They unhooked him from his tubes and put their arms around one side of Marvin, who suddenly had an upward-trend feeling. The three of them began to fly to heaven.
Marvin felt perfect serenity and a sense of excitement, with a profound sense of lightness and calm. The ride was smooth and wonderful, perhaps lasting a few seconds to a couple of minutes. They flew through a brilliantly blue sky.

He landed on solid ground in front of a massive,

monumental gate. He was in a line with about 35 other people of all nationalities. Color bursts lit the sky. He felt strong and fantastic.

Marvin heard music that was beyond compare. There was a choir of millions, with thousands of instruments that sounded like organs and pianos. Since then, every day he was on earth he heard bits of that music.

The colors and lights were deep, rich, glorious, and lush. The lights were indescribable. They were radiant and robust yet soft and delicate. It was like a laser show and like 10,000 silent fireworks going off at once.

Marvin saw babies, children, and grown-ups of all different ages playing, talking, and laughing.

The grass was the greenest he had ever seen. The skies and firmament were bluer than you could believe. The colors seem to incorporate the unique light of the sun, moon, stars, and fire, all in one.

Besteman had been dropped off by angels at heaven's gate. He saw an enormous door, several stories tall, and a wall that wrapped around the kingdom in either direction. The doorway was made of wood grain, almost like a rich mahogany, with a beautiful design in it.

"I found that many times I just knew things in heaven without being told . . . You just know what you know when you're there, and I knew this was a doorway."[2]

The 35 people in line with Besteman were smiling, with a deep, thorough contentment. The line was a melting pot of cultures and costumes, with people from all over the world and in all kinds of different clothing. There were many nationalities, including Scandanavian, Asian, African, and Middle Eastern.

Besteman knew for sure he had a redeemed body. "I felt like a teenager again, vital, awake and alert, strong and healthy as a horse."[3]

A man opened the door and stuck out his hand as his eyes lit up.

"Hello, Marv, my name is Peter. Welcome to heaven."

Besteman describes Peter as "humble and down-to-earth" and "just like a fisherman, with a scrubby beard, shaggy hair, and clothes that looked like he had been wearing them for 1,000 years of hauling in nets and gutting fish."[5]

Inside the massive doorway to heaven, there was an area like an inner gate. There was a long stone shelf extending to the left and right, on which books were stacked. The stones were like gray ash stone still standing today in parts of the world, such as the Middle East.

The shelf was about three feet high, and the books on it were about two and a half inches thick, about ten inches wide and 12 inches long, bound in ancient black cowhide, worn and antiqued. When Peter began looking through one of the books for Marvin's name, the latter realized these were the Books of Life.

Peter opened up one book and looked exactly where Besteman's name was to be, and it was not there.

Peter looked at the Book of Life for about 30 to 40 seconds. Just a few feet away, a glasslike gate rose upward and disappeared into a mist, like the stone shelf did. Behind Marvin, the dark wood gate also vanished in a swirl of filmy vapor. This gate was the gate of heaven.

There was a lake, and in the middle of Marvin's view, he saw some old fishing boats on the shore. Marvin could not see the lake's other side.

Peter told him "Marv, I can't find your name for today."[6]

Marvin actually asked Peter to look again for Marvin's name and even argued that his name should be there.

Outside the gate, Marvin pressed close to the gate and stared in at the surreal, beautiful realm before him. He saw things he will never forget. He pushed and pulled the gate and even pulled down on a steel beam, but nothing happened.

Beyond the gate, he saw millions of babies, from unborn to preterm to full term, and every age on up. He knew in his spirit that these babies had come to heaven when their lives had ended on earth. And he knew they would grow and be safe, happy, and loved.

No one needed to hold the babies, because the young ones were lying almost on "air pillows," a layer of space between them and the green grass below.[7]

Besteman saw six people in heaven. First he saw his grandparents Grace and Adrian Besteman, who were inside and saw Marvin. His grandmother smiled and waved, Marvin waved back, and his Grandpa motioned for Marvin to come in.

Then he saw his mother, who looked robust and healthy. She smiled a beautiful smile at her son and waved, and Marvin waved back.

He then saw two friends, Paul and Norm. They too smiled and waved for Marvin to come through the gate.

Marvin also saw his son-in-law Steve, a very close friend on earth. Steve had died in 2006 from a rare disease.[8]

THIRTY-ONE

Eben Alexander

Dr. Eben Alexander is a neurosurgeon in North Carolina, USA, where he lives with his wife and children.

In 2008, Alexander was experiencing a health crisis when he began his supernatural experience.

At first, he went into a visible darkness, as if he were submerged in mud that he could see through. It was blurry and suffocating. He felt as if he were conscious but with no idea of who he was.

There was a sound, a "deep, rhythmic pounding, distant yet strong."[1] It was almost mechanical, like a blacksmith hammering in the distance, with the vibrations going through the earth.

The word that came to mind later was "primordial."[2]
His language, emotion, and logic were gone. Wherever he was, he felt like he had always been there and would always continue there.

Eben recalls pondering that he might not survive, but the possibility did not bother him.

At some point, he became aware of objects around him which looked like roots or blood vessels, bloody and red.

Thinking back to this place, he named it the Realm of the Earthworm's-Eye View.

Analyzing this experience later, he realized that in this place, he was not human or animal. He felt like a point in a timeless sea.

The longer he was there, the more uncomfortable he became. At first he was immersed in this creepy world and did not feel any different from the surrounding elements. But this immersion turned into a feeling of being trapped.

The time stretched way out. The more he became aware of himself, the more the faces bubbling out of the darkness became ugly and threatening.

The rhythmic pounding sharpened and intensified, like a beat for an army of troll-like laborers. Eben began to feel the objects moving around him, rubbing against him with smooth or spiky skins. He was now aware of a smell, a mixture of feces, blood, and vomit.

Dr. Alexander was edging toward panic.

As he wondered how he would get out of this place, a beautiful entity approached him. He writes: "If I tried for the rest of my life, I would never be able to do justice to this entity that now approached me . . . to come anywhere close to describing how beautiful it was."[3]

This "something" radiated fine filaments of white-gold light, and the darkness around him began to break apart.

Next Eben heard "a living sound, like the richest, most complex, most beautiful piece of music you've ever heard."[4] It destroyed the pounding noise.

The light got closer and closer, a pure white light tinged with hints of gold. As Eben focused on the center of the light, he looked through it and began to move up very fast, with a whooshing sound. In a flash, he found himself in a completely new world, "the strangest, most beautiful world I'd ever seen."[5]

Eben uses words like "brilliant, vibrant, ecstatic, stunning" to describe the world, yet all words fall short. He felt like he was being born.[6]

He saw a countryside, green, lush, and earthlike. It was earth yet not earth. To Eben, it was like returning to a place you had been as a child, realizing that, though you do not think you remember it, you start to realize, deep down in your being, that you do know the place. You rejoice at being there.

Eben was flying, passing over trees, fields, streams, waterfalls, and people. He saw children laughing and playing. The people sang and danced in circles. At times he would see a dog, right in the middle of the people, as full of joy as the people were.

The people wore simple clothes that seemed to have "the same kind of living warmth as the trees and flowers that bloomed and blossomed in the countryside."[7]

The place was like an incredible dream world. However, Eben was absolutely sure of one thing: the place was real.

In this new place, time—like everything else—was different and impossible to describe. While flying, he realized he was not alone.

Next to him was a beautiful girl with deep blue eyes, wearing a gown like the people in the village below wore. They were riding along on a type of surface, alive with colors. There were millions of butterflies all around.

The girl's look of purity and genuineness was so special that, according to Eben, if you saw for just a few moments, it would you're your whole life up to that point worth living. He explains that it was a love beyond, higher, and more pure that all types of earthly love.

The colors of the girl's outfit had the same super-vivid, incredible aliveness that everything else had.

The girl spoke to Eben without using words, the message going to his core instantly. The message had three parts, about being loved, having nothing to fear, and doing no wrong. He felt a sensation of relief, like he understood the rules of life fully and completely.

The girl communicated another message to him: that she and others would show Eben many things, and that he would go back.

The next experience was even better.

Eben was in a place of clouds, which were big, puffy, and pink-white. The sky against them was deep blue-black.

Above the clouds, he saw beings he had never seen before. They were in flocks, shimmering across the sky. Somehow, these beings were more advanced and higher than others.

A glorious sound came down from above. Eben realized that these beings were so full of joy that they produced these sounds that were almost tangible, like a rain that does not get you wet.

Eben could hear and see the beauty and perfection of the beings. He felt like someone there would become a part of it, naturally and mysteriously. Somehow, everything there was distinct yet also part of everything else, "like the rich and intermingled designs on a Persian carpet . . . or a butterfly's wings."[8]

A warm wind blew and shifted everything to a higher level.

Eben asked questions and received answers instantly, in explosions of love, light, and color that did not need verbal words. He understood concepts that would take years on earth to comprehend.

During this experience, Eben explains that he actually visited three worlds, which he named: the Realm of the Earthworm's-Eye View, the Gateway, and the Core. The Gateway is his name for the green, brilliant, wonderful place with people. The Core is a "holy darkness."[9] Surprisingly, he was able to go back and forth "any number of times" among the realms.

A truth he received was that it would be impossible to understand it all, either the physical or spiritual dimensions or the "countless other universes."[10]

But even greater was the truth that "love is . . . the basis of everything."[11] Eben emphasized that it was love in its purest form: unconditional.

Later, in December 2008, Eben visited his Episcopal

Church, lit a candle for Advent wreath, and walked down to the altar. He writes: "I didn't just believe in God; I knew God."[12] Tears streamed down his cheeks.

An important part of the narrative is Eben's open and honest discussion and analyzation of being adopted as a child and his quest to reconnect with his birth parents.

After many years of attempting to meet his birth family, members of his birth family finally communicated with him. At the end of the book, Eben relates a full circle story. His birth sister Kathy had sent him a photo of his birth sister Betsy. At first he did not recognize it, but Eben soon realized that during his supernatural experience, the little girl he met is the "heavenly self" of Betsy.

THIRTY-TWO

Crystal McVea

In 2009, 33-year-old Crystal McVea died for nine minutes and had a supernatural experience. McVea, a mother of four children, was in the hospital suffering from a painful condition called pancreatitis when she had her near death experience. McVea is from Oklahoma, USA.

The moment she closed her eyes on earth is the moment she opened them in heaven. She no longer had a physical body and was now a spirit form. She had the stunning realization that she was the same person who had existed for all of eternity, long before her time on earth.

For McVea, no human words come close to describing the experience she had in the heavens.

Crystal was aware of her guardian angels and instantly knew them and loved them. Everything around her was of God: the light, the brightness, the angels, the communication. His radiance overwhelmed every sense that she had. She believes we have many senses in heaven.

She experienced a beautiful new way of receiving and sending love.

Her spirit soared, and her heart burst. She was in the presence of the Creator of the universe.

The communicaton between Crystal, the angels, and God was effortless and instant. There were open channels between them that allowed for the free flow of voluminous amounts of information.

Her questions and doubts disappeared. She understood that God's plan was perfect.

She did have one question, for herself: why didn't I do more for you?

The question was part of the divine communication between them, allowing them to be connected and infusing her with His love. Before she could voice a question, God gave her the answers.

She was naturally humbled and wanted to address her shortcomings on earth.

The Crystal and the angels went down a tunnel, a passageway of blinding brightness, guiding them to something. They came to the end of the tunnel, where they found the gates of heaven. It was the entrance to heaven.

God told her that once someone gets there, they cannot come back.

Crystal realized it was not her time to go in.

THIRTY-THREE

Robert Misst

Bob Misst is a prophetic intercessor and prayer warrior. He has ministered throughout India and now serves in his native New Zealand. His seminars "Worship, Warfare, and Intercession" prepare people for the return of the Lord Jesus. Before he met Jesus, Misst was an atheist.

During a prayer retreat in New Zealand, Bob suddenly realized he could no longer hear the worship music. He was being escorted from a tunnel of darkness toward a bright light. An angel's hand was on his right shoulder.

As he got closer to the light, he noticed large angels flying around a massive area. Seeing the countenance and size of the angels brought the fear of God into him. There was something holy about them. He realized his own sinfulness.

God's beings began speaking to him—not to his ears but to "the center of my head, like a spiritual download straight to [his] brain."[1] He knew he was in the courts of the heavenly temple of God.

The whole place was exuberant with the holiness of God. The angels sang "Holy, Holy, Holy is the Lord, who was and is and is to come." The escorting angel told him those angels were the cherubim, "the guardians of the Mercy Seat of God."[2] Bob was afraid of the cherubim. He felt that they were so filled with the mind of God and the intent to do His will that they could disintegrate his entire being into nothingness. They had multiple pairs of wings. The temple seemed to reverberate with their voices.

He then saw a group of people in stately attire. The group's body language was of holiness, love, humility, passion for God, and dedication in their service to Him. They wore crowns and looked like humans. They were the 24 elders.

Beyond the elders was a vast, innumerable crowd of people, seemingly billions times billions. They created a holy anticipation of the One who was to be in their midst. Their body language expressed a deep love, holiness, and passion for the One they worshipped. The angel said they were from every tribe, tongue, and nation. There were myriads of angels just above them, a sight that filled Bob with awe.

These sights reminded Misst of his dirty garments. The angel pressed Bob's shoulder, letting him know he was with Bob. It was imparted to Bob that the angel's mission was to escort Misst here and show him around.

In the center of this massive gathering of people was a bright light and an outline of a throne. Bob could barely discern the throne. There was a circular rainbow like a halo above the throne. When God and His Son, Jesus, entered the throne room, the atmosphere around the throne had the tangible holiness of God, with flashes of lightning and peals of thunder.

The cherubim flew around God's mercy seat. Bob could barely discern and perceive the outline of the mercy seat. When Moses built the Ark of the Covenant, the wings of the cherubim covered the mercy seat of God.

Bob was in awe of the exquisite beauty in the throne room, including unique shapes he had never seen or imagined. Objects even emitted sound and color and had the ability to resonate with heavenly music based on harmonies from our voices.

Suddenly, he was able to hear the worship. Bob felt like if he was in his mortal body, he could die just from the beauty of the sounds.

Then, he was in the throne room. He was overwhelmed. He heard the billion voices singing in seven-layered multiple chorus choirs. He saw sounds and colors as well as the lightning and thunder. The cherubim sang their song: "Holy, Holy, Holy is the Lord." The various choirs all sang in perfect harmony. There were instruments he had never seen.

A figure emerged from the light of the throne. It was Jesus.

Bob was filled with the fear of God. The 24 elders threw their crowns on the ground before Him and prostrated themselves there. He lifted them to their feet, in gentleness, love, and mercy. The Lord and the elders gazed at each other, with profound expressions of love, honor, respect, and holiness. Jesus put their crowns back on their heads.

The Lord Jesus interacted with the elders and even placed a crown on one of the other people there. Bob was moved and inspired to see Jesus lowering Himself and serving others.

The angel taught Bob that all worship in heaven has a purpose, one of which is to "move the end-time purposes of God on earth."[3] The seven groups in heaven have choruses that have a message for the church. They are:

The song of the cherubim – "Holy, Holy, Holy, is the Lord God, the Almighty, who was and who is and who is to come."

The song of the elders – "Worthy are You, our Lord and our God, to receive glory and honor and power; for You created all things, and because of Your will they existed and were created."

The song of the bride – the declarations by the nations about the beauty of the Lord and desiring to be with Him: "The Spirit and Bridge say, 'Come.'"

The song of the angels – the new song of heaven is "Worthy is the Lamb who was slain to receive power and riches and wisdom and might and honor and glory and blessing."

The song of the tribes and nations – "To Him who sits on the throne and to the Lamb be praise and honor and glory and power, forever and ever!"

The song of creation – "Salvation belongs to our God!"

The great thanksgiving song – "Hallelujah!"[4]

Bob then witnessed the Lamb of God taking the scroll and breaking the first seal. The elders communicated with Jesus, who seemed to be waiting "to hear the voice of His bride on the earth asking Him to come soon to the earth."[5]

A mighty cherubim called out, "Come forth," and a white horse with an angelic rider stood in front of the assembly.[6] The Lamb broke four seals amid worship and warfare.

Four horses with angelic riders appeared. The horses were white, red, black, and pale green.

Suddenly the lights in the heavenly temple went out, and Bob found himself back in the prayer room with the others staring at him. He opened his eyes.

Bob now understands the vision part better, as the Lord has released revelation about it. He joins in worship, warfare, and intercession, participating in the prophetic. Misst feels that Jesus wants His people to participate in what He is doing for the restoration and renewal processes of the church.

Notes

Cover Pages
1. Prince, Davis. *Nine Days in Heaven*, p. 15
2. Bennett, *To Heaven and Back*, p. 84
3. Hagin, *I Believe in Visions*, p. 50
4. Malz, My Glimpse of Eternity, p. 97
5. Eby, *Caught Up Into Paradise*, p. 199-200
6. Eby, *Tell Them I am Coming*, p. 73
7. Bennett, *To Heaven and Back*, p. 45
8. Liardon, *We Saw Heaven*, p. 28
9. Ibid., p. 51-52
10. Sigmund, *My Time in Heaven*, p. 41-42
11. Ibid., p. 86
12. Baxter, *Divine Revelation of Heaven*, p. 84-85
13. Buck, *Angels on Assignment*, p. 51
14. Ibid., p. 46
15. Bennett, *To Heaven and Back*, p. 62
16. Duplantis, *Close Encounters of the God Kind*, p. 114
17. Maelo, *Heaven and Back*, p. 41

Chapter 1 Marietta Davis
1. Prince, Davis. *Nine Days in Heaven* p. 5, 2. p. 6, 3. p. 8, 4. p. 10, 5. p. 13, 6. p. 15, 7. p. 15, 8. p. 15, 9. p. 19, 10. p. 19, 11. p. 20, 12. p. 21, 13. p. 22, 14. p. 26, 15. p. 27, 16. p. 29, 17. p. 34, 18. p. 37, 19. p.

37, 20. p. 38, 21. p. 53, 22. p. 58, 23. p. 120

Chapter 2 Rebecca Springer

Chapter 3 Lorraine Tutmarc
1. Bennett, *To Heaven and Back*, p. 83, 2. p. 84, 3. p. 84, 4. Kent and Fotherby, *The Final Frontier*, 5. Bennett, p. 95

Chapter 4 George Ritchie
1. Ritchie, *Return from Tomorrow*, p. 40, 2. p. 40, 3. p. 52, 4. p. 59, 5. p. 71

Chapter 5 Kenneth Hagin
1. Hagin, *I Believe in Visions*, p. 44, 2. p. 44, 3. p. 44, 4. p. 45, 5. p. 47, 6. p. 48, 7. p. 49, 8. p. 50, 9. p. 52

Chapter 6 Betty Malz
1. Malz, *My Glimpse of Eternity*, p. 97, 2. p. 99, 3. p. 99

Chapter 7 Deborah O'Donnell
1. Bennett, To Heaven and Back, p. 52, 2. p. 52

Chapter 8 Gary Wood
1. Roth and Lane, Heaven is Beyond Your Wildest Expectations, p. 23, 2. p. 28, 3. p. 29, 4. p. 30, 5. p. 31, 6. p. 36

Chapter 9 Richard Eby
1. Eby, *Caught Up Into Paradise*, p. 199-200, 2. Eby, *Tell Them I am Coming*, p. 73, 3. *Tell Them*, p. 73-74, *Caught Up*, 204-205, 4. *Caught Up*, p. 205, *Tell Them*, p. 70-71, 5. *Caught Up*, p. 205-206, 6. *Caught Up*, p. 202, 7. *Tell Them*, p. 68, 8. *Caught Up*, p. 204, 9. *Caught Up*, p. 202, 10. *Tell Them*, p. 68-70, 11. *Caught Up*, p. 203, 12. *Tell Them*, p. 73, *Caught*, p. 203-204, 13. *Tell Them*, p. 73, 14. Caught Up, p. 206, 15. Tell Them, p. 75, 16. Caught Up, p. 207-208, 17. Tell Them, p. 81-82, 18. Tell Them, p. 31-32, 19. Tell Them, p. 33-34, 20. Tell Them, p. 30

Chapter 10 Rhoda Jubilee Mitchell
1. p. 62, Roth, 2. p. 63, ibid., 3. p. 64, 4. p. 65, 5. p. 67, 6. p. 68, 7. p. 72, 8. p. 73-74, 9. p. 75-76

Chapter 11 Valvita Jones
1. Bennett, To Heaven and Back, p. 45, 2. p. 46, 3. p. 47, 4. p. 47, 5. Ibid.

Chapter 12 Roberts Liardon
1. *We Saw Heaven* p. 27, 2. p. 28, 3. *I Saw Heaven*, p. 26, 4. We Saw p. 27, 5. I Saw, p. 25, 6. p. 30, We Saw, 7. p. 30, 8. I Saw, p. 34-37 9. We Saw, p. 51-52, 10. p. 57, 11. p. 59, 12. p. 63, 13. p. 65, 14. p. 66

Chapter 13 Richard Sigmund
1. Sigmund, *My Time in Heaven*, p. 13, 2. p. 13, 3. p. 19, 4. p. 20, 5. p. 24, 6. p. 26, 7. p. 28-29, 8. p. 32-36, 9. p. 38-43, 10. p. 44-49, 11. p. 50-53, 12. p. 54-56, 13. p. 59, 14. p. 60, 15. p. 62-66, 16. p. 67-69, 17. p. 71-73, 18. p. 76, 19. p 78, 20. p. 78-81, 21. p. 86, 22. p. 82-86, 23. p. 88, 24. p. 87-89, 25. p. 92-94, 26. p. 96, 27. p. 99-101, 28. p. 104, 29. p. 105-112, 30. p. 114-115, 31. p. 126-127

Chapter 14 Mary Baxter
1. Baxter, Divine Revelation of Hell, p. 14, 2. p. 17, 3. p. 17-19, 4. Stories of the SuperNatural", 5. "Stories," Hell, p. 26-28, 6. Hell, p. 32-38, 7. p. 45-48, 8. p. 50-54, 9. p. 56, p. 55-57, 10. p. 59-70, 11. p. 72-73, 12. Revelation 21:3, 13. Revelation 21:4-5, 14. 4-5, 14. p. 74-76, 15. "Stories," Hell p. 80-82, 16. "Stories," Hell p. 84-86, 17. P. 85-90, 18. "Stories," Hell p. 99, 19. p. 103-112, 20. p. 113-118, 21. p. 124-125, 22. p. 126-129, 23. p. 133-136, 24. 163, 168

Chapter 15 Roland Buck
1. Buck, *Angels on Assignment*, p. 15, 2. p. 61, 3. p. 15, 4. p. 15, 5. p. 23, 6. p. 24, 7. p. 29, 8. p. 40, 9. p. 41, 10. p 44, 11. p. 44, 12. p. 165, 13. p. 166-171, 14. p. 51, 15. p. 51, 16. p. 51, 17. p. 51-52, 18. p. 52, 19. p. 52-53, 20. p. 55, 21. p. 54-57, 22. p. 56, 23. p. 57, 24. p. 59, 25. p. 59-61

Chapter 16 Gerald Landry
1. Bennett, *To Heaven and Back*, p. 58-59, 2. P. 60, 3. P. 60, 4. P. 61, 5. P. 61, 6. P. 61, 7. P. 62, 8. P. 62, 9. P. 62

Chapter 17 Ian McCormick
1. NationalGeographic.com, 2. Roth, Heaven is Beyond Your Wildest Imagination, p. 84, 3. p. 87, 4. p. 88, 5. p. 89, 6. p. 90

Chapter 18 Yong Gyu Park
1. Park, "Donate All of His $150 Million US Dollars"

Chapter 19 Jesse Duplantis
1. Duplantis, p. 54, 2. p. 69, 3. p. 69-71, 4. p. 72, 5. p. 73, 6. p. 74, 7. p. 78, 8. Ibid, 9. p. 81, 10. p. 83, 11. p. 85, 12. p. 88, 13. p. 90, 14. Ibid, 15. p. 93, 16. Ibid, 17. p. 94, 18. Ibid, 19. p. 97, 20. p. 98, 21. p. 100, 22. p. 101, 23. p. 102, 24. p. 103, 25. p. 106-107, 26. p. 108, 27. Jonah, 3:10, 28. p. 109, 29. p. 113, 30. p. 114, 31. Ibid, 32. Ibid, 33. p. 117, 34. Ibid, 35. p. 119, 36. p. 120, 37. p. 121, 38. p. 122, 39. p. 125, 40. Revelation 21:4-5, 41. p. 127-128, 42. p. 132, 43. p. 117

Chapter 20 Don Piper
1. Don Piper, *90 Minutes in Heaven*, p. 22, 2. p. 31, 3. p. 22-36

Chapter 21 Choo Thomas
1. Choo Thomas, *Heaven is So Real!*, p. 54, 2. p. 62, 3. p. 72-73, 4. Revelation 22:7, 5. p. 120

Chapter 22 Maurice Maelo
1. Maurice Maelo, *Heaven and Back*, p. 18, 2. p. 19, 3. p. 20, 4. p. 22, 5. Ibid, 6. p. 28, Revelation 4:10, 7. p. 29, 8. p. 30, 9. p. 41, 10. Ibid, 11. p. 45

Chapter 23 Khalida Wukawitz
1. "Story of Khalida," 2. Roth, *Heaven is Beyond Your Wildest Imagination*, p. 1063. P. 107, 4. Ibid., 5. P. 108, 6. P. 109, 7. P. 110, 8. Ibid.

Chapter 24 Bill Smith
1. Roth, *Heaven is Beyond Your Wildest Imagination* p. 154, 2. p. 155, 3. p. 151-156

Chapter 25 Mary Neal
1. CBN, Neal, "Drowning Victim's Visit to Heaven." 2. CBN, Neal, 3. Neal, *To Heaven and Back*, p. 56, 4. Neal, p. 58, 5. CBN, Neal, 6. Neal, p. 68, 7. Neal, p. 71, 8. p. 70, 9. p. 70, 10. p. 73

Chapter 26 David Taylor
1. Taylor, *My Trip to Heaven*, p. 157, 2. p. 158, 3. p. 162, 4. Matthew 10:32, 5. p. 167, 6. Ibid., 7. p. 168, 8. p. 169, 9. p. 170, 10. Ibid., 11. p. 177

Chapter 27 Michael McCormick
1. Roth, *Heaven is Beyond Your Wildest Imagination*, p. 101, 2. p. 102, 3. p. 97-102

Chapter 28 Colton Burpo
1. Burpo, *Heaven is For Real*, p. xvii, 2. p. xxi, 3. p. 54, 4. p. 59, 5. p. 63, 6. Ibid., 7. p. 65, 8. Ibid., 9. Ibid., 10. p. 76, 11. p. p. 71, 12. p. 75, p. 13, p. 76, 14. p. 95, 15. p. 100-104, 16. p. 106-107, 17. p. 132, 18. p. 136-138

Chapter 29 Dean Braxton
1. Roth, p. 39, 2. p. 41, 3. Braxton, "My Visit to Heaven," 4. p. 44, 5. Ibid., 6. Braxton, "My Visit to Heaven," 7. Roth, p. 54

Chapter 30
1. Besteman, *My Journey to Heaven*, p. 13, 2. p. 74, 3. p. 78, 4. p. 103, 5. Ibid., 6. p. 117, 7. p. 129, 8. p. 55-129

Chapter 31 Eben Alexander
1. Alexander, *Proof of Heaven*, p. 29, 2. p. 30, 3. p. 32, 4. p. 38, 5. Ibid., 6. p. 39, 7. Ibid., 8. p. 46, 9. p. 70, 10. Ibid., 11. p. 71, 12. p. 148

Chapter 32 Crystal McVea
1. CBN, "Nine Minutes in Heaven," McVea, *Waking Up in Heaven*

Chapter 33 Bob Misst
1. Roth, *Heaven is Beyond Your Wildest Imagination*, p. 118, 2. p. 119, 3. p. 126, 4. p. 126-127, 5. p. 127, 6. p. 128

Bibliography

Prince, Dennis and Nolene, Davis, Marietta. *Nine Days in Heaven* (Lake Mary, FL: Creation House-Strang, 2006).

Scott, J.L. *Scenes Beyond the Grave* (Dayton, OH: Stephen Deuel, 1859), public domain.

Spring, Rebecca Ruter. *Intra Muros* (BiblioLife LLC).

Springer, Rebecca. *Within Heaven's Gates* (New Kensington, PA: Whitaker House, 1984).

Kent, Richard, and Fotherby, Val. *The Final Frontier* (The Final Frontier Charitable Trust).

FreeChristianTeaching.org

Rawlings, Maurice S. *Beyond Death's Door* (Nashville, TN: Thomas Nelson Inc., Publishers, 1978).

Bennett, Rita. *To Heaven and Back* (Grand Rapids, MI: Zondervan, 1997).

Ritchie, George G., *Return from Tomorrow* (Grand Rapids, MI: Revell, Baker Book House Company, 1978).

Moody, Raymond S. *Life After Life* (New York: HarperCollins, 1975, 2001; MBB, Inc, Bantam Books).

Hagin, Kenneth E. *I Believe in Visions* (Tulsa, OK: Rhema Bible Church, 1984).

Malz, Betty. *My Glimpse of Eternity* (Grand Rapids, MI: Revell/Baker Publishing Group, 1977).

Wood, Gary. *A Place Called Heaven* (Mustang, OK: Tate Publishing & Enterprises, LLC, 2008).

Roth, Sid and Lane, Lonnie. *Heaven is Beyond Your Wildest Expectations* (Shippensburg, PA: Destiny Image Publishers, Inc., 2012).

GaryWood Ministries.org

Eby, Richard E. *Caught Up Into Paradise* (Grand Rapids, MI: Revell/Baker Book House Company, 1978).

Eby, Richard E. *Tell Them I am Coming* (Grand Rapids, MI: Revell/Baker Book House Company, 1980).

Mitchell, R. Jubilee. *Journey of Comfort* (2004).

Jones, Valvita. "Remember to Love." SeattleLANDS Newsletter, November-December 1992.

Liardon, Roberts. *We Saw Heaven* (Shippensburg, PA: Destiny Image Publishers, Inc., 2000).

Liardon, Roberts. *I Saw Heaven* (Tulsa, OK: Albury Publishing, 1983).

Sigmund, Richard. "A Place Called Heaven." The Lord's Hour Radio Show, Leicester, NC.

Sigmund, Richard. *My Time in Heaven* (New Kensington, PA: Whitaker House, 2004).

Baxter, Mary. "Stories of the SuperNatural," Interview. YouTube.com/watch?v=15Zvh7qCKJ0

Baxter, Mary K. with Lowry, Dr. T. L. *A Divine Revelation of Heaven* (New Kensington, PA: Whitaker House, 1998).

Baxter, Mary K. *A Divine Revelation of Hell* (New Kensington, PA: Whitaker House, 1993).

Buck, Roland. *Angels on Assignment* (Kingwood, Texas: Hunter Books, 1979).

White, Sharon Rose. *The Man Who Talked With Angels* (Boise: Heartbeat Ministries).

Buck, Roland. "Angelic Visitations" Audio (Boise, ID: Central Assembly of God, 1979).

Park, Yong Gyu. "Donate All of His $150 Million US Dollars After He Visited Heaven and Hell- Yong Gyu Park". YouTube.com/watch?v=wXmALH5eS9k

Duplantis, Jesse. "Close Encounters of the God Kind" Testimony, YouTube.com/watch?v=SEJNJp_pXVc.

Duplantis, Jesse. "Heaven in Real!" YouTube.com/watch?v=GUJI6hZtFeE.

Duplantis, Jesse. *Close Encounters of the God Kind* (Tulsa,

OK: Harrison House, 1996).

Piper, Don. "90 Minutes in Heaven." YouTube.com/watch?v=D5w7a0zf-d8

Piper, Don. *90 Minutes in Heaven* (Grand Rapids: Revell/Baker Publishing Group, 2004).

Thomas, Choo. *Heaven is So Real!* (Lake Mary, FL: Charisma House, 2003).

Maelo, Maurice. *Heaven and Back* (South Africa: Kairos Media & Publications, 1999).

Wukawitz, Khalida, Youtube Channel, YouTube.com/channel/UCwBEPdH7OnVj3ayUSheEscQ

Wukawitz, Khalida, "Story of Khalida," YouTube.com/watch?v=Yp1sotupPHg

Neal, Mary. "Drowning Victim's Visit to Heaven." (Christian Broadcasting Network, 2012). youtube.com/watch?v=7LNT8NHfxec

Neal, Mary. *To Heaven and Back* (Colorado Springs, CO: Waterbrook Press, 2011).

Taylor, David. *My Trip to Heaven* (Shippensburg, PA: Destiny Image Publishers, Inc., 2011).

Burpo, Todd with Vincent, Lynn. *Heaven is For Real* (Nashville, TN: Thomas Nelson Inc., 2010).

Braxton, Dean. *In Heaven* (Good Book Publishing, 2009).

Braxton, Dean. "My Visit to Heaven."v Sid Roth's It's Supernatural. YouTube.com/

watch?v=kGQPQ2EJVyY.

Besteman, Marvin. *My Journey to Heaven* (Revell: Baker Publishing Group, 2012).

Christian Broadcasting Network, "Nine Minutes in Heaven-Crystal McVea (Testimony)," January 2, 2014. YouTube.com/watch?v=8JEz3tEWXXs

McVea, Crystal and Tresniowski, Alex. *Waking Up in Heaven* (New York: Howard/Simon and Schuster, Inc., 2013).

Misst, Robert. *Worship, Warfare & Intercession*: Before the Throne of God (2011).

www.ingramcontent.com/pod-product-compliance
Lightning Source LLC
LaVergne TN
LVHW051550070426
835507LV00021B/2503